IN STORMS OF STEEL

ERNST JÜNGER (1920)

IN STORMS OF STEEL

ERNST JÜNGER

Translated and Edited by
K.J. ELLIOTT

ANARCH BOOKS
2022

Printed in the United States of America

English translation of *In Stahlgewittern: Aus dem Tagebuch eines Stoßtruppführers* by Ernst Jünger, published by E. S. Mittler & Son, Berlin, 1922.

Cover art: Robert Meier's cover illustration for the first edition of *In Stahlgewittern* (1920)
Cover design: K.J. Elliott

ISBN: 9798812659714

Anarch Books | www.anarchbooks.com

Preface

THE shadow of the monster still looms over us. The mightiest of wars is still too close to us for us to be able to survey it completely, let alone crystallize its spirit visibly. One thing, however, stands out more and more clearly from the flood of phenomena: the paramount importance of matter. War culminated in the battle of materials; machines, iron and explosives were its factors. Even man was counted as material. Formations were burnt to cinders again and again at the focal points of the front, withdrawn and subjected to a schematic recovery process. "The division is ripe for a major battle."

The image of war was sober, its colors gray and red; the battlefield was a desert of madness, where life eked out a meager existence underground. At night, weary columns of men rolled along crushed roads toward the blazing horizon. "Lights out!" Ruins and crosses lined the way. No song resounded, only soft words of command and curses interrupted the crunch of metal, the clatter of rifles against the clay walls. Blurred shadows emerged from the edges of crushed villages into endless trenches.

No regimental music surrounded companies marching into battle, as once in the past. That would have been a mockery. No flags floated as once through the gun smoke over chopped-up squares, the dawn did not shine on a happy horse-riding day, no chivalrous fencing and dying. The laurel seldom wreathed the brow of the worthy.

And yet, this war also had its men and its romance! Heroes, if the word had not become cheap. Daredevils, unknown, brazen fellows, who were not granted the privilege of being intoxicated by their own boldness in front of everyone. Lonely they stood in the storm of battle, when death galloped as a red knight with hooves of flame through flowing mists. Their horizon was the edge of a crater, their support was the sense of duty, honor, and intrinsic worth. They were conquerors of fear; rarely did they have the salvation of being able to look the enemy in the eye, after everything terrible had piled up to the last peak and had wrapped the world in blood-red veils. Then they rose to fierce greatness, lithe tigers of the trenches, masters of explosives. Then their primal urges raged with the most complicated means of destruction.

But even if the mill of war ran more quietly, they were still admirable. Their days were spent in the bowels of the earth, surrounded by mold, tortured by the eternal clockwork of falling water drops. When the sun sank behind jagged shadow-cracks of ruins, they escaped the pestilential breath of black caverns, resumed their burrowing work, or stood, like iron pillars, for nights behind the ramparts of trenches, staring into the cold silver of hissing flares. Or they crept as hunters over clicking wire into the wasteland of no man's land. Often sudden flashes of lightning tore through the darkness, shots rang out, and a shout drifted into the abyss. So they worked and fought, poorly fed and clothed, as patient, iron-laden day laborers of death.

Sometimes they came back, stood dreamily on the concrete seas of the cities, and looked incredulously at the life that flowed whirling in its normal courses. Then they threw themselves into the experience, so as not to let a minute of the short days pass unused, drank and kissed. With the recklessness that had become their way of life, they swung the cup in mad nights until the world fell away from them. Then they let their fallen friends live and didn't give a damn about the next day. And then it was back to the usual ways of the trench.

This was the German infantryman in war. No matter what he fought for, his struggle was superhuman. The sons had outgrown their people. With bitter smiles they read the trivial newspaper drivel, the worn-out words of heroes and heroic death. They didn't want that kind of thanks, they wanted understanding. No thanks can be big enough. A picture: the highest Alpine peak, a solemn face under a heaving steel helmet, looking silently and seriously across the land, down the German Rhine to the open sea. One day the day will come.

* * *

The purpose of this book is to give the reader a factual account of what an infantryman experienced as a rifleman and leader during the Great War in the midst of a famous regiment,[1] and what he thought about it. It has arisen from the contents of my war diaries put into form. I tried to put my impressions on paper as directly as possible, because I noticed how quickly impressions become blurred and how they take on a different coloration after only a few days. It took energy to fill this pile of notebooks, in the brief pauses of action, after the day's work at the front, by the dim light of a candle, on the stairs of narrow corridors, in tent-covered craters or the damp cellars of ruins; but it was worth it. I have preserved the freshness of the experiences. Man tends to idealize what he has achieved, to cover up what is ugly, petty and commonplace. Imperceptibly, he stamps himself as a "hero."

I am not a war correspondent, I do not present a collection of heroes. I do not want to describe how it could have been, but how it was.

Iliacos muros peccatur intra et extra.
(Sins are committed both inside and outside the walls of Troy.)

The degree of objectivity of such a book is the measure of its intrinsic value. War, like all human actions, is composed of good and evil. Only here, where the power of peoples rises to the highest, the contrasts stand out even more glaringly than usual. Next to culminating values, the darkest abysses yawn. Where one man reaches the almost divine level of perfection, the selfless devotion to an ideal to the point of sacrificial death, there is another who greedily picks the pockets of the barely dead. Those intoxicated by great words collapse miserably at the moment of danger. Men whose convictions seemed as solid as a rock put themselves "on the ground of facts" in a decisive hour, without drawing the sword that otherwise rattled so

---

[1] The parent regiment of the 73rd Fusilier Regiment, formerly the Royal Hanoverian Guard Regiment, defended Gibraltar victoriously against the Spanish and French for almost four years from 1779 to 1783 under General Elliot. To commemorate this glorious feat of arms, our regiment wears a blue ribbon with the inscription "Gibraltar" on the sleeve of its tunic. The same sign is now carried on by the 5th Company of the 16th Reichswehr Regiment (Hanover).

resoundingly. Others smolder through the nights in which the sky glows red and quiet droning beats admonishingly against the windows.

This must be said. Out of this dark background the true man stands out all the more brilliantly, the inconspicuous, genuine, spirit-driven warrior who did his duty on the last day as on the first. What was the frenzy of 1914 in comparison? A mass suggestion! And yet, how many have I met who, under the gray cloth, harbored a heart of gold and a will of steel, a selection of the most capable who threw themselves into the arms of death — with unchanging joy. Whether you have fallen in the open field, your poor face disfigured with blood and dirt by the enemy, surprised in dark caves or defeated in the mud of endless plains, crossless, lonely sleepers; this is gospel to me: you have not fallen in vain. Though perhaps the goal is another, greater than you dreamed. War is the father of all things. Comrades, your value is imperishable, your monument deep in the hearts of your brothers who stood with you, surrounded by the flaming ring. Didn't we put white ribbons on your wounds and look into your breaking eyes when the curtain of eternity rushed up to you?

May this book help to give an idea of what you have achieved. We have lost much, perhaps everything, including honor. One thing remains: the honorable memory of you, of the most glorious army that ever bore arms and of the mightiest war ever fought. To uphold it in the midst of this time of soft whining, moral atrophy and renegadeism is the proudest duty of everyone who fought for Germany's greatness, not only with rifle and hand grenade, but also with a living heart.

ERNST JÜNGER, 1920

Contents

I.   Orainville 1

II.   From Bazancourt to Hattonchâtel 8

III.   Les Éparges 12

IV.   Douchy and Monchy 18

V.   The Daily Positional Battle 27

VI.   Prelude to the Battle of the Somme 38

VII.   Guillemont 54

VIII.   At St. Pierre-Vaast 68

IX.   The Somme Retreat 75

X.   In the Village of Fresnoy 80

XI.   Against the Indians 89

XII.   Langemarck 101

XIII.   Regniéville 120

XIV.   Return to Flanders 129

XV.   The Battle of Cambrai 139

XVI.   At the Cojeul River 151

XVII.   The Great Battle 155

XVIII. English Advances 179

XIX.   My Last Storm 192

I

Orainville

THE train stopped in Bazancourt, a small town in Champagne. We got off. With incredulous awe, we listened to the slow, rhythmic drum roll in the front, a melody that was to become very familiar to us in the long years to come. A white cloud of shrapnel melted far away in the gray December sky. The breath of battle hovered all around, giving everyone a strange chill. Did we realize then that that dark rumbling behind the horizon, growing into an incessant rolling thunder, would end up swallowing us all whole, first one and then another?

We had left the lecture halls, school desks, workshops; and in a few short weeks of training we had fused together to form a large, enthusiastic body, bearers of the German ideals of the post-eighteen seventies. Growing up in the spirit of a materialistic time, the longing for the unusual, for the great experience, was woven in us all. Then the war had seized us like a powerful intoxication. In a rain of flowers, we had gone out in a drunken Morituri mood. The war had to bring it to us, to the great, the strong, the solemn. It seemed to us a manly deed, a cheerful gunfight on flowery, blood-covered meadows. There is no more beautiful death in the world.... Oh, don't just stay at home, come join in!

"Fall in in a group column!" The heated imagination calmed down while marching through the heavy clay soil of Champagne. Knapsack, cartridges, and rifle weighed like lead. "Shorten the steps. Stay up back there!"

> Ah, the spirit's wings will soon be
> No physical wing to join!

1

Finally we reached the village of Orainville, the resting place of the 73rd Fusilier Regiment, one of the typical nests of that area, formed by fifty little houses made of brick and clay around an isolated castle in the middle of a park. The hustle and bustle of the main village street presented a strange and unusual sight to eyes accustomed to city culture. One saw only a few shy and ragged civilians; everywhere were soldiers in worn, tattered coats with weather-beaten faces, mostly framed by large beards, strolled along at a slow pace or stood in small groups in front of the doors of the houses and welcomed us newcomers with stinging jokes. Somewhere there was a field kitchen with pea soup, surrounded by food fetchers clattering with cookware. The Wallensteinian romanticism was heightened by the incipient decay of the village.

After spending the first night in a massive barn, Lieutenant von Brixen, the colonel's adjutant, assigned us to the various units in the castle courtyard. I was assigned to the 9th Company.

Our first day of war was not to pass without leaving a decisive impression on us: we were sitting in the school assigned to us as quarters, eating breakfast. Suddenly, a series of dull thuds rang out nearby, while soldiers rushed toward the village entrance from every house. We followed this example without quite knowing why. Again, a strange, never-before-heard fluttering and roaring sounded overhead, drowning in rumbling crashes. I was surprised that the people around me huddled together as if under a terrible threat.

Immediately after, groups blackened by dust and smoke appeared on the deserted village street, on stretchers or dragging black bundles with their firmly clasped hands. With a strangely suffocating feeling of unreality, I stared at a soldier covered in blood with his leg hanging loosely from its body, incessantly shouting a hoarse "help!" and being carried into a house from whose entrance the Red Cross flag was waving. What had happened? The war had shown its claws and thrown off its cozy mask. It was so mysterious, so unreal. One could hardly think of the enemy, that enigmatic, treacherous being somewhere back there behind the horizon. The event, which was completely outside of experience, made such a strong impression that it took effort to grasp its exact meaning. It was like the appearance of a ghostly apparition at noon.

A grenade had exploded up there against the entrance of the castle, hurling a hail of stones and shrapnel into the entrance just as the occupants, startled by the first shots, were pouring out of the gateway. Thirteen people were killed, including the music master Gebhard, a familiar figure to me from the Hanover promenade concerts. A tethered horse sensed the danger sooner than the men, tore itself loose a few seconds before and galloped into the castle courtyard without being injured.

In conversation with my comrades I noticed that this incident had very much dampened the enthusiasm for war in some men. That it had also had a strong effect on me was evident from numerous auditory hallucinations, which transformed the rolling of every passing car into the fatal sound of the ill-fated grenade.

In the evening of the same day, the long-awaited moment came when, heavily packed, we set out for the battle position. Through the ruins of the village of Bétricourt, towering out of the fantastic semi-darkness, our way led us to a lonely forester's lodge, hidden in the fir woods, the so-called "Pheasantry," where the regiment's reserves were located, to which the 9th Company, lying there, also belonged until that night. Their leader was Lieutenant Brahms.

We were received, distributed among the platoons, and soon found ourselves in a circle of bearded, clay-encrusted men who welcomed us with a certain ironic goodwill. We were asked how life was in Hanover and whether the war would soon be over. Then the conversation returned into monotonous brevity about the trenches, field kitchens, trench sections and other matters of positional warfare.

After some time the call rang out in front of the door of our sort of hut: "Everyone out!" We joined our groups and at the command: "Lock and load!" with a secret lust we thrust live rounds into the magazine.

Then we walked silently, man after man, across the nocturnal landscape dotted with dark patches of forest. Every now and then a lone shot would ring out, or a flare would fizzle out to leave an even deeper darkness after a brief, ghostly illumination. Monotonous clatter of rifle and trench gear interrupted by the warning cry, "Watch out, barbed wire!" How often after that first time I would stroll through destroyed landscapes to the front line in a half melancholy, half excited mood!

Finally, we disappeared into one of the trenches that wound like a white snake through the night to the battle position. There I found myself lonely and shivering between two parapets, staring anxiously into a row of fir trees lying in front of the trench, in which my imagination conjured up all kinds of shadowy figures, while now and then a stray bullet would crack through the branches. The only change in this seemingly endless time was that I was partnered up with an older comrade and trotted with him through a long, narrow corridor to a sentry box, where we were again busy looking at the foreground. Finally, for two hours, I was able to abandon myself in the bottom of a hole to the sleep of exhaustion. When morning dawned, I was pale and clay-covered like the others, and I felt as if I had been living this mole's life for months.

The regiment's position described a curved line on the clay soil of Champagne, opposite the village of Le Godat. It leaned to the right against a copse decimated by bombings, the so-called "Grenade Forest," then ran through huge beet fields from which stood out the red of the pants of those who had fallen in the last battle, and ended in a creek bottom across which communications with the 74th Regiment were maintained by night patrols. The stream rushed over the barrage of a ruined mill surrounded by dark, sinister trees. An eerie sojourn, when, at night, the moon, coming out of a crack in the clouds, made fantastic shadows appear while strange noises seemed to mix with the murmur of the waters and the rustling of the reeds.

The service was the most exhausting imaginable. Life began with the onset of dusk, during which the entire crew had to stand in the trenches. From 10 o'clock in the evening until 6 o'clock in the morning two men of each group were allowed to sleep, so that one enjoyed a night sleep of two hours, which was reduced, most of the time, to a few minutes, due to an early wake-up call.

Either one had to stand guard in the trench, or one moved into one of the numerous outposts, connected to the position by long, shallow walkways dug into the limestone; which was soon abandoned during the positional battles, since such positions held very little protection.

These endless, terribly tiring night watches were still bearable in clear weather and even in frost, but they became agonizing when it rained, as it usually did in January. When the dampness penetrated first the canvas pulled over one's head, then the coat and uniform, and trickled down the body for hours, one fell into a mood that could not be lightened even by the rumbling of the approaching relief. The dawn illuminated exhausted, clay-smeared figures who threw themselves, teeth chattering, with pale faces on the rotten straw of the dripping shelters. These shelters! They were nothing more than holes dug in the limestone, with an opening in the wall of the trench, covered with boards and a few shovels of earth. After the rain, the water would drip into them for days on end; with dubious humor, someone would put handwritten signs above the entrance, saying "Dripstone Cave," "The Men's Shower," etc. In order for several people to rest in it at once, one was forced to stretch one's legs out in the dugout, thus creating an inevitable trap for those who passed through. Under these circumstances, of course, one could not even talk about resting during the day. In addition, there was the two-hour guard duty, the cleaning of the trench, fetching food, coffee, water and other things.

One will understand that this unaccustomed life seemed very hard to us, especially since we were also harassed in every way by most of the veterans. This habit, which we had brought with us from the barracks into the war, contributed a great deal to making the hard days even harder for us, but it disappeared after the first battle we had fought together. The common soldier also found it difficult to understand the fact that we had volunteered. He saw it as a certain arrogance, a view I often encountered during the war.

The time when the company was in reserve was not much better. We then lived in fir branch-covered earth huts near the Pheasantry or in Hiller's grove, whose dung-packed floor at least radiated a pleasant fermenting warmth. Sometimes one woke up in an inch-deep puddle of water. Although I had only known rheumatism by name, after a few days of permanent bathing I felt excruciating pain in all my joints.

The nights were not used for sleep, but for deepening the numerous access trenches.

A bright spot in this dreary monotony was the arrival every evening of the field kitchen at the corner of the Hiller grove, where a delicious aroma of peas with bacon or other delightful things spread when the kettle was opened. But even here there was a dark point: the dried legumes, which were reviled by disappointed gourmets as "canned barbed wire" or "hunting pellets."

The most pleasant days were the rest days in Orainville, which were spent sleeping in, cleaning clothes, and drills. The company lived in a huge barn that had only two chicken ladder-like staircases for entry and exit. Although the building was still filled with straw, there were stoves inside. One night, in my sleep, I rolled toward one of these stoves until I touched it; the energetic action of my companions to extinguish it woke me up. I noticed, however, with great disappointment that the back of my uniform had been considerably blackened; I went around, for some time, wearing a sort of tailcoat.

After a short stay with the regiment, we had lost almost all the illusions with which we had set out. Instead of the dangers we had hoped for, we had found dirt, work and sleepless nights, the conquest of which required a heroism that was unsuited to our nature. This constant overexertion was the fault of the leadership, which had not yet grasped the spirit of the new type of positional warfare. In a short, daredevil battle, the officer can and must ruthlessly exhaust the crew; in a long, dragged-out war, this leads to physical and moral collapse. The enormous number of posts and the uninterrupted trench work was for the most part unnecessary and even harmful. The important thing is not the power or solidity of the trenches, but the courage and efficiency of the men behind them. "Iron hearts on wooden ships win the battles."

We heard the whistling of bullets in the trenches and occasionally received a few grenades from the Reims forts, but these little incidents of war events fell far short of our expectations. Nevertheless, we were sometimes reminded of the bloody seriousness that lurked behind these seemingly unintentional events. On January 8th, for example, a grenade struck the Pheasantry and killed the adjutant of the battalion commander, Lieutenant Schmidt.

On January 27th, in honor of our Emperor, we sounded three powerful hurrahs and sang "Heil dir im Siegerkranz" (Hail in victory) on the long front, accompanied by a heavy barrage from enemy rifles.

During these days I had a very unpleasant experience, which almost brought my military career to a premature and inglorious end. The company was located on the left wing. One morning, with another soldier, after having kept watch all night, I descended to the bottom of the valley for double sentry duty. Because of the cold, I had wrapped my blanket around my head and was leaning against a tree, and placed my rifle next to me in a bush. Suddenly I heard a noise behind me, reached for it — the gun was gone! The inspection officer, who had slipped silently behind me, had taken it from me without my noticing anything. As a punishment, he sent me, armed only with a trench shovel, to within a hundred yards of the French sentries. An Indian idea that almost got me killed. During that strange punitive vigil of mine, in fact, a patrol of three volunteers crossed through the reeds, shaking them so carelessly that they were immediately noticed by the French and fired upon. One of them, named Lang, was hit and never seen again. Since I was standing close by, I took my share of the fire, and the willow branches, under which I was carefully concealed, lashed my ears. I gritted my teeth and remained motionless out of defiance. I have never been able to forget the utter meanness of this deputy officer.

We were all heartily proud when we were told that we were to leave this position for good, and we celebrated our departure from Orainville by having a hearty beer party in the big barn. On February 4, 1915, relieved by a Saxon regiment, we marched to Bazancourt.

This month was for me, although the hardest of the war so far, nevertheless a good educational experience. I had become thoroughly acquainted with guard duties and trench labor in its most difficult form. Later, when I was in charge, this saved me from asking the impossible of my men.

II

From Bazancourt to Hattonchâtel

IN Bazancourt, a desolate village in Champagne, the company took lodging in the school to which, due to the amazing sense of order of our people, soon took on the appearance of a peacetime barracks. There was a non-commissioned officer on duty, who woke us up punctually in the morning, the corps leaders were on parlor duty, and every evening there was a roll call. Every morning the companies moved out to drill for a few hours on the nearby wastelands. After a few days I was taken away from this duty by being sent to the Officer Aspirant Course in Recouvrence.

Recouvrence was a remote village hidden in lovely limestone hills where a number of young people were sent by the division to receive thorough military training from an officer and a few NCOs provided by each regiment. We of the 73rd Regiment owe much in this regard to the extremely capable Lieutenant Hoppe, who unfortunately died shortly thereafter.

Life in this remote nest consisted of a strange mixture of barracks drill and academic freedom. During the day, the students were honed into military men using every trick in the book; in the evening, they gathered with their teachers around huge barrels, where they caroused just as thoroughly. When the various sections streamed out of their pubs in the morning hours, the small houses took on the unusual appearance of a German university's hustle and bustle. Incidentally, our course leader, a captain, had the educational habit of handling the duty on the following days with double the energy.

Our intercourse with each other was very cordial, as was natural among people of the same educational level under these circumstances. We lived in groups of three or four and took our meals together. Of our daily meal I have the best memories, especially of scrambled eggs and fried potatoes. On Sundays we were treated to a rabbit or a rooster. I was in charge of the purchases for the evening meal: and it was in this capacity that I was presented one fine day, by our landlady, with a series of vouchers that she had received from soldiers as receipts for requisitions, a true anthology of popular humor: for the most part they said that Fusilier XY had granted his favors to the landlady's daughter and had been forced to requisition a dozen eggs to restore his strength. Unfortunately, this delightful anthology of folk humor is too juicy to be quoted here.

In mid-February, we of the 73rd Regiment were painfully struck by the news of the heavy losses suffered by the regiment at Perthes, and we regretted having spent those days far from our comrades. On March 21st, having passed a small examination, we returned to the regiment again stationed at Bazancourt. A few days later, after a big parade and a farewell speech by General von Emmich, the unit was detached from the 10th Corps. We were loaded on March 24th and proceeded to the Brussels area, where with the 76th and 164th Regiments, we formed the 111th Infantry Division.

Our battalion was housed in the small town of Hérinnes (Flemish: Herne), in the middle of a landscape of Flemish comfort. I experienced my 20th birthday here quite happily.

Although the Belgians had plenty of room in their houses, our company, out of false consideration, was put into a large drafty barn through which the rough sea wind of that area whistled during the cold March nights. Otherwise, our stay in Herne was quite restful; there was a lot of drill, but there was also good rations and cheap food.

The population, half Flemish and half Walloon, was very friendly to us. I often conversed with the owner of a café, a zealous socialist and free spirit, who invited me to a feast on Easter Sunday and would not even accept money for all of the drinks. One can hardly imagine how beneficial such an encounter is in the midst of the rough school of field comradeship.

Towards the end of our stay, the weather became beautiful and invited us to take walks in the lovely, watery surroundings. The landscape was picturesquely decorated by the many undressed men-of-war who, their laundry on their laps, eagerly hunted for lice along the poplar-lined banks of the stream. Having been spared from this plague so far, I helped my war comrade Priepke, a Hamburg export merchant, to wrap a heavy stone in his woolen vest, which was populated like the jacket of "Simplicissimus," and lowering it to the bottom of a stream. Since our departure from Herne was very sudden, the vest is probably still enjoying an undisturbed stay there today.

On April 12, 1915, we were loaded into Hal and, in order to deceive spies, drove across the northern wing of the front to the area of the Mars-la-Tour battlefield. The company moved into its usual barn quarters in the village of Tronville, one of the usual boring Lorraine dirt nests made up of flat-roofed, windowless stone boxes. Because of the danger of airplanes, we had to stay mostly in the crowded village, near which are the famous sites of Mars-la-Tour and Gravelotte. A few hundred meters from the village, the road to Gravelotte was cut by the border, where the French border post laid shattered on the ground. In the evenings we often took the wistful pleasure of a walk to Germany.

Our barn was so dilapidated that one had to balance in order not to fall through the rotten boards onto the threshing floor. One evening, while our group, with the good Corporal Kerkhoff, was dividing up the rations, a huge oak beam broke loose from the scaffolding and fell with a great crash. Fortunately, it wedged itself between two mud walls just above our heads. We escaped with a fright, but our nice portion of meat had been rendered inedible by the whirled-up debris. We had hardly settled down on this ominous evening when there was a heavy thunder of knocks at the door and the alarming voice of the sergeant drove us from the camp. At first, as always in such moments, a moment of silence, then a confused, loud commotion: "My helmet!" "Where is my haversack?" "I can't get my boots on!" "You stole my magazines!" "Shut up!"

Finally, we were ready and marched to Chamblay station, from where we reached, with a few minutes by train, Pagny-sur-Moselle. We climbed the heights of the Moselle during the morning and stopped at Prény, a delightful mountain village topped by the ruins of a castle. This time our barn was a stone structure filled with aromatic mountain hay, from whose hatches we could look out over the vine-covered Moselle mountains and the little town of Pagny, down in the valley, which was often pounded with shells and aerial bombs. A few times a shell hit the Moselle river, sending up a towering column of water.

The warm weather and the magnificent landscape had a truly invigorating effect on us and encouraged us to take long walks during our free time. We were so high-spirited that we joked for some time in the evening before everything quieted down. Among other things, it was a popular joke to pour water or coffee from a canteen into the mouths of snorers.

On the evening of April 22nd, we left Prény and, after a march of more than thirty kilometers, we reached the village of Hattonchâtel without having a single man crippled despite the considerable weight of the heavy baggage; we camped on the right of the famous Grande Tranchée (Grand Trench) right in the middle of the forest. It was obvious from all the signs that we would be in the action the next day. We received medical dressing packs, a second ration of meat cans and signal flags for the artillery.

In the evening, I sat for a long time in that foreboding mood, of which warriors of all times know too well, on a tree stump overgrown with blue anemones, before I crawled over the bodies of the other comrades to my campsite. During the night I had confused dreams in which a human skull played the most important role. Priepke, to whom I told about the dream the next morning, hoped that it had been a French skull.

III

Les Eparges

THE young green leaves of the forest shimmered in the morning light. We wound our way through hidden paths to a narrow ravine behind the front line. It was announced that the 76th Regiment was to storm after twenty minutes of fire preparation and that we were to stand by as a reserve. At 12 o'clock sharp our artillery opened a fierce cannonade, which echoed many times in the forest canyons. For the first time we understood the true meaning of the harsh expression "fire at will." We sat on our knapsacks, idle and excited. An orderly rushed to the company commander with hasty words. "The first three trenches are in our hands, six guns captured!" A cheer flared up. A daredevil mood arose in the men.

Finally, the longed-for order came. We moved forward in a long line, from where indistinct gunfire cracked. It became serious. To the side of the forest path, dull thuds rumbled in a fir thicket, branches and earth rained down on us. A fearful man threw himself to the ground amid forced laughter from his comrades. Then the exhortation of death slid through the ranks, "Medics to the front!"

On the Grande Tranchée, troops rushed forward. Wounded men begging for water huddled at the roadside, prisoners carrying stretchers were walking in the opposite direction, galloping drums were banging amidst the gunfire. Shells pounded the soft ground on the right and left, heavy branches came crashing down. In the middle of the road laid a dead horse with huge gaping wounds, next to it steaming entrails. Leaning against a tree was a bearded reservist: "Now get a move on, boys, the Frenchman is on the run!"

We entered the battle-scarred realm of the infantry. The surroundings of the position were deforested by shells. In "no man's land," entirely devastated, the victims of the attack were all lying with their faces pointed in the direction of the enemy, with their gray uniforms barely distinguishable from the ground. A gigantic figure, his face framed by a red, blood-stained beard, looked at the sky with motionless eyes, his hands stuck in the soft earth. A boy was twisting in the hole dug by a grenade: he had the earthy color of death on his face. Our glances seemed to irritate him; with an indifferent gesture he pulled his coat over his head and kept silent.

We broke away from the marching column. Shells continually hissed over in a long, sharp arc, lightning swirled up the ground of the clearing. "Medic!" We had the first casualty. Fusilier S. had his carotid artery torn apart by a shrapnel bullet. Three bandage packs were soaked in an instant. He bled to death in seconds. Next to us two guns blazed away, attracting even heavier fire. An artillery lieutenant, searching for wounded in the area in front of us, was thrown to the ground by a grenade explosion. A large column of smoke suddenly rose in front of him. He got up slowly and returned with an incredible calm. "Just developed quite the stagger!" Our eyes gleamed at him admiringly.

It was dark when we received the order to advance. Our path led us through dense, bullet-riddled undergrowth into an endless running trench that fleeing Frenchmen had strewn with equipment. Near the village of Les Eparges, with no troops in front of us, we had to take up a position by digging into solid rock. At last, I sank into a bush and fell asleep.

"Get up, we're moving out!" I woke up in dew-damp grass. Through the whizzing sheaf of a machine gun, we rushed back into the trench and occupied an abandoned French position at the edge of the woods. A sweet smell and a bundle hanging in the wire entanglement caught my attention. I jumped out of the trench in the morning mist and stood before a shriveled French corpse. The decomposed fish-like flesh stood out with its greenish-white color in the tattered uniform. As I turned back, I recoiled in horror: a human figure was crouched against a tree beside me. Two empty eye sockets and a few tufts of hair on his blackish-brown skull revealed to me that I was not dealing with a living person. All around laid dozens of corpses, decomposed, calcified, dried into mummies, frozen in an eerie dance of death. The French must have held out for months next to their fallen comrades without burying them.

In the morning hours the sun broke through the fog and sent out a cozy warmth. After sleeping a bit on the trench bottom, I walked through the lonely trench stormed the day before, its floor covered with mountains of provisions, ammunition, equipment, weapons and newspapers. The shelters resembled looted junk stores. Between them laid the corpses of brave defenders, their rifles still stuck in the embrasures. A jammed torso protruded from a shot-up entablature. Head and neck had been cut clean off the body, white cartilage gleamed from reddish-black flesh. The entire scene was very disorienting. Next to it, a very young person on his back, his glassy eyes and fists frozen in the aiming position. A strange feeling to look into such dead, questioning eyes. A shudder that I never quite lost during the war. Next to him laid his poor, plundered purse.

With increasing clarity, the artillery fire intensified and soon increased to a wild dance. I returned to my group. In shorter and shorter pauses it flared up around us. White, black and yellow clouds mingled in the air. Sometimes blasts of a terrifying percussive force resounded, followed by flares making the sound of strange canary chirps. Soon the forest was ablaze, flames climbing up the trees with a crackling sound. I was sitting with a comrade on a bench cut into the clay of the trench wall, while next to us a gaunt recruit was trembling with fear in all his limbs. My companion made the cruel joke of secretly hurling a handful of shrapnel balls next to him.

I watched the forecourt with a peculiar calm. "They don't even know where you are. They can't even see you, they're shooting somewhere else entirely." It was the courage of inexperience. Suddenly the board of the embrasure thumped, and an infantry bullet slammed into the clay between our heads. At that moment a man appeared at the corner of our trench section, "Follow to the left!" We passed on the order and strode along the smoke-filled position. Just then the food haulers had returned and abandoned hundreds of steaming cans of food in the trench. Who could eat at a time like this? A crowd of wounded with blood-soaked bandages pressed past us, the excitement of battle on their pale faces. The foreboding of a particularly critical hour loomed before us. "Look out, comrades, my arm, my arm!" "Go, go, man, hold the line!"

The trench ended in a wooded area. Indecisively, we stood under huge beech trees. Our platoon leader, a lieutenant, emerged from the dense undergrowth and shouted to the oldest sergeant, "Have them fan out toward the setting sun and take position. Inform me at the shelter by the clearing." Cursing, the sergeant executed the command.

The impression this behavior made on the men was a powerful lesson for me throughout my time as a leader. Later I got to know this officer, who still often distinguished himself, as a comrade and learned that he had important things to do. No matter what, the officer must under no circumstances separate himself from the crew when in danger. Danger is the noblest moment of his profession, and it is there that he must prove his enhanced manliness. Honor and chivalry elevate him to the master of the hour. What is more sublime than to advance a hundred men to their death? Such a personality is never denied allegiance, the courageous deed flies through the ranks like an intoxication.

We scattered and lay in wait in a series of shallow holes already dug by someone. The jokes we were exchanging were suddenly interrupted by a bloodcurdling roar that made us all shudder. Twenty meters behind us clods of earth came whirling over from a white cloud, slapping through the high branches of the trees. Many times the sound echoed through the forest. Dazed eyes stared at each other, bodies nestled against the ground in a depressing feeling of complete helplessness. Shot followed shot. Deadly gases seeped into the bushes; heavy smoke enveloped the tops of the trees; trunks and branches broke down amidst high screams that rose all around. We jumped high and ran blindly, rushed by lightning and stupefying air pressure, from tree to tree, seeking cover and circling around huge trunks like hunted game. A shelter into which many ran received a direct hit that tore up its thick wood beam decking.

I hurried around a mighty beech tree with the sergeant, panting. Suddenly there was a flash of lightning in the far-reaching roots, and a blow against my left thigh threw me to the ground. I thought I had been hit by a clod of earth, but the abundant flow of blood soon showed me that I had been wounded. It later became apparent that a razor-sharp splinter had struck me in my upper leg after its force had been softened by my thick leather purse.

I threw away my haversack and ran toward the trench from which we had come. Wounded men were streaming out of the shelled copse from all sides. The entrance was a horrible sight to behold, blocked by the seriously wounded and the dying. A body naked to the waist, with a torn back, was leaning against the wall. Another, with a triangular flap hanging down from the back of his skull, was uttering high-pitched, nerve-shattering cries. And still more impacts.

I will openly confess that my nerves left me completely in the lurch. I had to get away, further, further! Recklessly, I ran over everything. I am not a friend of the euphemism: nervous breakdown. I was afraid, pale, simply terrified. I often thought back to those moments later, shaking my head.

Nearby was a log-covered medical shelter where I spent the night, cramped in with the many wounded. An exhausted doctor stood in the midst of the throng of groaning bodies, bandaging, giving injections and recommendations in a soothing voice. When I was being carried away the next morning, a splinter pierced the canvas of the stretcher right between my knees.

I was transported across the still heavily shelled Grande Tranchée to the main dressing station and then to the church in the village of St. Maurice. Next to me in the hammered hospital wagon laid a man with a shot in the belly who pleaded with his comrades to shoot him with the medic's pistol. In St. Maurice a hospital train was already under steam, which would transport us to Heidelberg in two days. At the sight of the Neckar hills crowned by blossoming cherry trees, I felt a peculiar, strong sense of home. How beautiful the country was, well worth bleeding and dying for.

The battle of Les Eparges was my first. It was very different from what I had thought. I had taken part in a major war operation without having really seen the enemy at all. It was only much later that I experienced the clash, the culmination of modern combat in the appearance of the infantryman in the open field, interrupted for a few decisive, murderous moments in the chaotic emptiness of the battlefield.

IV

Douchy and Monchy

MY wound was healed in two weeks; I was discharged to the reserve battalion in Hanover and enlisted there as an ensign. After attending a course in Döberitz and being promoted to ensign, I returned to the regiment in September 1915.

I left the train with a small reserve detachment at the headquarters of the division, the village of St. Léger, and marched to Douchy, the regiment's resting place. In front, the autumn offensive was in full swing. On this immense battlefield, the front was drawn like a long, billowing line of clouds. The machine guns of the air squadrons rattled over our heads. An observation balloon seemed to have spotted us, at the entrance to the village the black smoke of an exploding grenade sprang up in front of us. I turned and led the column of men into the village by another route.

Douchy, the resting base of the 73rd Fusilier Regiment, was a village of medium importance, and had suffered very little from the war. This place, situated in the undulating terrain of the Artois, became the regiment's second garrison during its year and a half of fighting in that area, a place of rest and inner consolidation after hard days of fighting and work in the front line. How often we breathed a sigh of relief when, through the dark rainy nights, a lonely light gleamed at us from the entrance to the village! We had a roof over our heads again and a simple, undisturbed camp. We felt reborn when on the first day of rest we bathed and scraped the mud of the trenches off our uniforms. The surrounding meadows were used for drill and exercising to get the rusty bones limber and to reawaken the feeling of togetherness among the men who had been lonely during the long night watches. All this gave us strength for the hard, tiring days ahead. In the early days, the companies took turns marching to the front line for nightly entrenchment work. This overly burdensome double occupation was later abandoned by order of our Lieutenant Colonel von Oppen. The security of a position is guaranteed by the freshness and reserves of courage of its defenders, and not by the labyrinth of its approaches or the depth of its trenches.

In the free hours, Douchy offered its gray uniformed inhabitants more than one source of entertainment. Many cellars were still abundantly stocked with provisions and beverages; there was a library, a café, and there was even a movie theater, ingeniously installed in a giant barn. The officers had their clubhouse and a field for playing skittles in the garden of the rectory. Company parties were often celebrated during which officers and troops challenged each other to solemn drinking, according to the good old German custom.

Since the civilian population still lived in the village, the available space had to be utilized in every way. Barracks and living quarters had been built in the gardens; a large orchard in the center of the village had been turned into a church square, another, the so-called Emmich Square, into an amusement park. At Emmich Square, in two shelters covered with tree trunks, were the shaving parlor and the dental station. A large meadow next to the church served as a burial ground, to which a company marched almost daily to pay its last respects to one or many comrades to the sound of a choir.

The French population was all gathered at the exit of the village on the Monchy side. Most of them were shy, pitiful figures who had to bear the brunt of the war. Unsuspecting children played in front of the doors of the dilapidated houses, and the elderly men dragged themselves curtly through this unusual animation that alienated them with a brutal ruthlessness from the places where they had spent their lives. The young people were obliged to present themselves at roll call in order to be sent, by the commander of the square, Lieutenant Oberlaender, to the various work groups in charge of cultivating the fields of the village. We only met with the locals when we brought them our laundry to be cleaned or to buy eggs and butter. Delicate relationships were extremely rare; eroticism found no room in the desolate, disruptive gears.

One of the strange things that happened in this small military town was the adoption by the troop of two French orphans. These little boys, one of whom must have been eight years old and the other twelve, were both dressed in gray cloth and spoke fluent German. As for their compatriots, they only knew them by the name of "Schangels" which they had learned from our soldiers. Their most fervent wish was to one day be able to go in line with "their" company. They knew the exercises to perfection, saluted their superiors, took their places on the left wing of the company during appeals and asked for regular permission when they wanted to accompany the adjutant to Cambrai for shopping. When the 2nd Battalion, after a few weeks, was sent to Quéant for instruction, one of them by the name of Louis was supposed to have remained at Douchy by order of Colonel von Oppen; so, during the march, no one saw him, but on the arrival of the battalion he cheerfully escaped out of the baggage wagon where he had been hiding. It seemed that the eldest was later sent to an ensign school in Germany.

Barely an hour's walk from Douchy was Monchy-au-bois, the village that housed the regiment's two reserve companies. In the fall of 1914, the place had been the scene of fierce fighting; finally, it now remains in our hands, and the battle waged in a semicircle around the ruins of this once wealthy village has slowly come to an end.

Now the houses were burned out and shot up, the overgrown gardens plowed by shells, the fruit trees broken. A tangle of large stones were set up for defense with trenches, barbed wire, barricades and concreted bases. Roads could be taken under machine-gun fire from a concrete square in the middle of an intersection, the so-called "Torgau Fortress." Another base was the "Altenburg Fortress," a field building to the right of the village where part of the reserve company was housed. A very important point of resistance was the tunnel of a stone quarry from which the limestone material used in the construction of the houses had been taken and which we had discovered by chance. One of the company cooks had dropped his bucket in a well; he lowered himself to the bottom and noticed a cavity that gradually widened until it became a cave. Having examined the place and created a second access, a large number of fighters were offered a large bomb-proof shelter.

On the isolated rise overlooking the Ransart road were the ruins of an old café that we had nicknamed "Bellevue" because of the wide view it offered of the front. I had a particular fondness for this place, even though it was dangerously exposed. The sad impression of the destruction made the abandonment and the deep silence more sensitive, interrupted from time to time by the deafening cannonade. Torn backpacks, broken rifles, shreds of cloth, and in the midst of them, a hideous contrast, a toy, grenade fuses, deep craters of exploded shells, bottles, harvesting tools, torn books, domestic furnishings, perturbations whose mysterious darkness revealed a cellar where perhaps the corpses of the unhappy inhabitants were being consumed by a pack of frantic rats, a small peach tree that, deprived of the supporting wall, stretched out its arms in supplication, animals carcasses still attached to the chain in the stables, graves in the wild garden and in the middle, barely discernible among the weeds, the green of onions, wormwood, rhubarb, daffodils, fields of wheat with sprouting ears of grains. Melancholic thoughts creep over the warrior whose foot rests on the ruins of such a site, when he remembers those who lived peacefully here only a short time ago.

The fighting position, as already reported, ran in a tight semicircle around the village, to which it was connected by a series of running trenches. It was divided into two subsections, Monchy-South and Monchy-West. These in turn were subdivided into six company sections A to F. The arched shape of the position provided the English with a good flanking opportunity, which was also duly exploited and brought us heavy losses.

I was assigned to the 6th Company and a few days after my arrival I moved into position as leader of a group, where I was immediately given an unpleasant reception by some English mines. Section C, where the company was located, was the most exposed of the regiment. However, in our company commander, Lieutenant (ret.) Brecht, who had hurried over from America at the beginning of the war, we had an officer who was the right man for defending such a position. His daredevil nature sought out danger and ultimately brought him a glorious death.

Our life in the trench was very orderly; I describe below the course of a normal day.

The day in the trench begins at dusk. At 7 o'clock a soldier from my group woke me up from my afternoon nap in anticipation of the night watch. I buckle up, put my flare gun and hand grenades in the belt and leave the more or less comfortable refuge. Walking through the familiar section of the train for the first time, I make sure that all the sentries are in their proper places. In a low voice the password is exchanged. In the meantime, night has fallen, and the first silvery flares rise into the air, while strained eyes stare into the foreland. A screeching rat rustles among the tin cans that were thrown over the cover. Then a second one joins it, and soon scurrying shadows swarm in from the village's ruined cellars or shot-up tunnels. Hunting them provides a popular distraction in the tedium of guard duty. A piece of bread, at which the rifle is pointed, serves as bait, or blasting powder from unexploded ordnance is scattered in their holes and set on fire. Squealing, they then shoot out with scorched fur. They are vile, disgusting creatures. A ghastly haze hangs around their buzzing packs. I always think about their hidden, corpse-devouring activity in the cellars of the village. A few cats have also moved from the ruined villages to the trenches; they love to be near people. A large white tomcat with a broken front paw often hangs around no man's land and seems to frequent both camps.

But I was talking about trench duty. One loves such digressions, one easily becomes talkative in order to occupy the dark night and the endless time. That's also why I always stop and visit with the well-known warriors or other NCOs and listen with eager interest to their insignificant meanderings. As an ensign, I am also often engaged in sympathetic conversation with the officer on watch, who is as equally uncomfortable as I am. Yes, he even becomes quite companionable, talks quietly and eagerly, discloses his secrets and desires. And I gladly go along with it, because the heavy, black walls of the trench also weigh on me, I also long for warmth, for something human in this eerie solitude.

The conversation becomes duller. We are tired. We lean tiredly against the wall and stare at each other's glowing cigarette. . . .

In frosty weather, one stamps up and down, freezing, so that the hard earth resounds under your footsteps. Very often it rains, then one stands sadly with the lapels of the coat raised under the canopy of the tunnel entrances and listens to the falling rain drops. If one hears the footsteps of a superior on the wet trench floor, one quickly steps out, continues walking, turns around suddenly, clicks his heels together and reports: "Sergeant on trench duty. Nothing new to report in the section!" Because standing in the shelter entrances is forbidden.

The thoughts wander. You look at the moon and think of beautiful, cozy days at home or of the big city far away, where people are streaming out of the cafes right now, and many arc lamps illuminate the lively, nocturnal hustle and bustle of the city center. Sometimes it seems as if this past life had only been a dream.

Something rustles in front of the trench, two wires clink softly. In an instant the dreams flutter away, all senses are sharpened to the point of pain. Someone climbs onto the post, shoots up a flare: nothing moves. It was probably only a hare or a partridge.

Often you can hear the enemy working on his wire entanglement. Then you shoot in the direction of the sound in quick succession. Not only because it's an order, but one also feels a certain satisfaction in doing so. "Now they're feeling the pressure. You might have even hit one." We also pull wire almost every night and often men are wounded in the process. Then we curse at those mean English pigs.

Occasionally, you can hear a hiss, a fluttering sound after a dull bang. "Look out, bomb!" You rush to the next tunnel entrance and hold your breath. Shells explode quite differently, much more exciting than the grenades. There is something so devouring, so sinister about them in general, a kind of demonic personality. They are insidious creatures. Rifle grenades are not much better. If it lights up in certain places of the enemy rear, all the sentries jump from their posts and disappear. They know from experience exactly where the guns are located, and which are pointed specifically at Section C.

Finally, the luminous dial shows that two hours have passed. I quickly wake up the relief and return to the shelter. Perhaps the men from Essenholt have brought letters, parcels or a newspaper. One feels quite a strange sensation when reading the news of home and its peaceful concerns, while the shadows of the fluttering candle flit across the low, rough timber beams. After scraping the coarsest dirt from my boots with a chip of wood and brushing it against one leg of the table, I stretch out on the cot, with the blanket pulled over my head, to take, as they say, a four-hour nap. Outside, bullets bang on our cover in monotonous repetition, a mouse scurries across my face and hands without disturbing my sound sleep. I am also at peace from the insects; we thoroughly fumigated the shelter only a few days ago.

Twice more I am roused from my sleep to perform my duties. During the last watch, a bright line in the eastern sky behind us announces the new day. The outlines of the trench become sharper; in the gray light of dawn it offers a spectacle of unspeakable desolation. A lark soars high; I find its squawking to be an intrusive contrast, it irritates me. Leaning against a crossbar, I stare at the dead wire-enclosed apron in a feeling of great disillusionment. The last twenty minutes don't want to end at all! At last, the cooking utensils of the returning coffee carriers clatter in the trench: it is 7 o'clock, the night watch is over.

I go to the shelter and drink coffee. That perks me up; I have lost the desire to lie down. At 9 o'clock I have to organize my group for work and get them in line. We are true handymen; the trench makes its thousand demands on us every day. We dig deep tunnels, build concrete shelters, prepare wire obstacles, create drainage systems, formwork, shore, level, raise and slope, fill latrines, and so on.

At 1 o'clock, lunch is brought out in large containers, former milk jugs and jam buckets, the rations were brought from the kitchen set up in a cellar in Monchy. After the meal we sleep or read a little. Gradually, the end of the two hours of day watch are approaching. They pass significantly faster than those of the night. One observes the well-known enemy position with binoculars or with a trench periscope and often you have the opportunity to shoot with a precision rifle equipped with a scope, a weapon reserved for head shots. But one has to be careful, even the Englishman has sharp eyes and good scopes.

A guard suddenly collapses, covered in blood. Shot in the head. The comrades tear the bandages off his coat and bandage him up. "It's no use, Willem." "Man, he's still breathing!" Then the paramedics come to carry him to the dressing station. The stretcher bumps hard against the angled crossbar. As soon as it disappeared everything goes back to normal. Someone throws a few shovels of earth over the pool of blood and everyone goes about their business. One has become so desensitized. Only one new recruit is still leaning against the wooden cladding of the wall, distraught, with a pale face. He is still struggling to grasp the context. It was so sudden, so terribly surprising, an act of indescribable brutality. It can't be possible, it can't be real. Poor guy, he'll be seeing a lot worse than this!

It can also be quite nice. Some of them are interested in the hunt. They view the impacts of their own artillery in the enemy trench with a certain glee. "Boy, I got that one." "Golly, look at that splash! Poor Tommy!" They enjoy shooting rifle grenades and mortars across, much to the chagrin of the anxious minds. "Gee, cut the nonsense, we've got enough trouble already!"

The hour of the afternoon coffee can sometimes even be enjoyable. The midshipman is often, in this case, the guest of an officer of the company. It is quite formal: "May I have your permission?" "Thank you obediently!" A beautiful quality of the Prussian officer, this proper uniformity in every situation. It even gives the young soldiers something firm, personal.

There are two porcelain cups that stand out on the sackcloth tablecloth. The attendant sets a bottle and two glasses on the unstable table. The conversation becomes more confidential. Oddly, even here it is the neighbor who becomes, more often than not, the favorite topic of conversation. A lavish trench gossip has even developed, which is eagerly cultivated during the afternoon rounds. Soon it's like being in a small garrison. Superiors, comrades and subordinates are subjected to minute criticism. A new rumor makes the rounds of the shelters and commands in no time, in all six sections, from the right wing to the left wing. The observation officers, who walk the entire regimental position with telescope and sketch folder, are not entirely innocent in this.

"Mr. Lieutenant, allow me to say goodbye, I'm on duty in half an hour!" Outside, the last rays of the sun gleam into the mud walls of the embankments, the trench is already in a deep shadow. Soon the first illuminating flare will rise, the night sentries will take their place, and a new day of the trench soldier will begin.

V

The Daily Positional Battle

OUR days passed in a painful monotony, interrupted by brief periods of rest at Douchy. Even in the trenches, however, good times were sometimes experienced. Often I sat with a feeling of comfortable security at the table of my small hut, whose rough, weapon-covered plank walls reminded me of the Wild West, drank a cup of tea, read and smoked, while my orderly was busy at the tiny stove, which filled the room with the smell of toasted bread. What trench warrior doesn't know this mood? Outside, in front of the guardhouse, heavy, regular footsteps could be heard echoing; monotonous calls rose as the sentries crossed into the trench. The slightly weakened hearing could barely perceive the incessant rifle fire, the brief impact of the bullets against the defenses or the hissing of the flare which, once the illuminating charge had been used up, gradually weakened until it was extinguished. Then I took my notebook out of the map pocket and wrote down in short words the events of the day. Thus, over time, a conscientious chronicle of Section C, that small, angular piece of the long front in which we were at home, in which we had long known every trench hidden in grass, every dilapidated shelter, came into being. Around us, in piled-up mounds of clay, rested the corpses of fallen comrades, on every foot of ground a drama had taken place, behind every parapet lurked doom, day and night, ready to seize any victim indiscriminately. And yet we all felt a strong sense of belonging to our section, we were firmly attached to it. We knew it when it stretched like a black ribbon across the snow-covered countryside, or when, around noon, the flowering fields all around it flooded it with heady scents, or when the full moon wove ghostly paleness around its dark corners, where packs of squeaking rats did their mysterious bidding. We sat cheerfully on its clay benches on long summer evenings, when the balmy air carried bustling men and native songs to the enemy; we tumbled over timbers and barbed wire, when death beat the trenches with its iron club, and when idle clouds of smoke rose above the piles of crushed clay walls. The colonel tried to direct us to a quieter part of the regimental position several times, each time the whole company pleaded like a single body to be allowed to stay in Section C. I report here a short excerpt from the notes I wrote down during those nights at Monchy.

* * *

October 7, 1915. I was standing, at dawn, near the sentry of my group on the firing line in front of our shelter when a rifle bullet tore the man's field cap from front to back without so much as a scratch. A few minutes later, two sappers were wounded at the wire. One caught a ricochet shot through both legs, the other was shot through the ear.

In the morning, the sentry to the left received a shot through both cheekbones. Blood gushed in thick streams from the wound. To make matters worse, Lieutenant von Ewald came into our section today to photograph Sappe Unit N., which was only fifty meters from the trench. As he turned to climb back down from the guard post, a bullet shattered the back of his head. He died instantly. Furthermore, another man received a light shoulder shot.

October 19th — The middle section of the platoon was bombarded with fifteen centimeter shells. One soldier was thrown against a support poll of the trench lining by the air pressure. He suffered severe internal injuries, and a fragment also pierced his brachial artery. In the morning fog, while mending our wire in front of the right wing, we discovered a French corpse that must have been lying there for months. During the night two of our men were wounded while pulling wire.

October 30th — Last night, after a thunderstorm, all the parapets collapsed, mixing with the water from the rain in a slush that reduced the trench to a bottomless swamp. The only consolation was that the English were no better off, for water was seen being eagerly drawn from their trenches as well. Since we were somewhat elevated, we pumped our abundance of water down to them. The falling trench walls exposed a number of corpses from the previous fall's battle.

November 21st — I led a detachment of trench workers from the "Altenburg Fortress" into Section C, of which Diener, a member of the Landsturm Battalion, climbed a ledge of the trench wall to shovel earth over cover. No sooner was he on top when a bullet fired from the enemy trench went straight through his skull, dropping him dead on the trench floor. He was married and the father of four children. His comrades lurked behind the embrasures for a long time, seeking blood. They wept with rage. It is strange how little objectivity they had about the war. They seemed to see a very personal enemy in the Englishman who fired that fatal bullet. I can sympathize with them.

November 24th — A soldier of the M. G. K. (Machine Gun Company) was severely shot in the head in our section. Another soldier of our company had his cheek split open half an hour later by an infantry bullet.

* * *

On November 29th, our battalion was transferred for fourteen days to Quéant, a little town situated in the rear of the division, which would later gain a bloody reputation, in order to drill there and enjoy the blessings of the rear. During our stay there I received my promotion to lieutenant and was transferred to the 2nd Company, where I was to spend many serious and cheerful days.

In Quéant and the neighboring villages, we were often invited by the local commander to heavy drinking and got a small insight into the almost absolute power with which these village lords ruled over their subjects and the inhabitants. Our cavalry captain called himself the "King of Quéant" and appeared every evening, greeted by raising his right hands and a thunderous: "Long live the king," at the table, where he ruled as a whimsical majesty, à la Shakespeare, until the gray morning, punishing every breach of etiquette and his extremely complicated commentary with a compulsory round of beer. We front men, as newcomers, naturally came off very badly. The next day, after lunch, he was usually seen driving through his lands in a "Dogcart," slightly veiled, to pay his respects to the neighboring kings with a strong Bacchus offering and thus to prepare himself worthily for the evening. Once he got into a quarrel with the King of Inchy and had a mounted gendarme announce his declaration of war. After several battles, during which two detachments of horse groomers threw clods of earth at each other from small wire-fortified trenches, the King of Inchy was careless enough to feast on Bavarian beer in the canteen of the King of Quéant and was surprised, captured and taken prisoner. He had to buy his way out of jail with a huge ton of beer. Thus ending the feud of the two mighty men.

The inhabitants were subject to strict discipline, and violations and offenses were punished by the local commander in swift justice with severe fines and even imprisonment. As much as I am a supporter of the logical implementation of the idea of power, I was already disgusted and embarrassed by its excesses, such as the obligation of every inhabitant, including women, to greet the officers. Such regulations are pointless, degrading and harmful. But this is how we managed throughout the war: dashingly in trivial matters, indecisively in the face of serious internal damage.

On December 11th, walking in the open, I reached the front line to present myself to Lieutenant Wetje, commander of my new company, which, by rotation with my old 6th Company, now held Sector C. When I jumped into the trench I was struck by the changes that had taken place in the position during my fifteen days' absence. It had become, due to a few landslides, an immense pit full of mud in which the troop led, wading, a very sad existence. I thought back, melancholically, to the round table of the King of Quéant, while I was already up to my hips in sludge. Poor derelicts of the front that we were! Almost all the shelters had collapsed and the tunnels flooded. We worked breathlessly for the next few weeks trying to get our feet back on solid ground. While we waited, I lived with Lieutenants Wetje and Boje in a tunnel whose ceiling, in spite of the canvas we had spread underneath it, dripped like a watering can and from which the attendants had to remove the water in buckets every half hour.

When I left the tunnel the next morning, completely soaked, I could not believe my eyes. The terrain, which until then had been marked by the loneliness of death, had taken on the appearance of a fairground. The crews of both trenches had been driven onto the open terrain by the terrible mud, and already a lively traffic and exchange of liquor, cigarettes, uniform buttons, etc., had developed in front of the wire entanglements. The crowd of khaki-colored figures that spilled out of the hitherto so barren English trenches had a directly astounding effect.

Suddenly a shot rang out from the enemy side, causing one of our men to fall dead in the mud, whereupon both parties disappeared back into the trenches like moles. I went to the part of our position opposite the English column and shouted that I wanted to speak to an officer. Sure enough, some Englishmen went back and after a short time brought with them a young man who, as I could observe through the glass, was distinguished from them by a daintier cap. We negotiated at first in English, then somewhat more fluently in French, while all the men around listened. I reproached him with the fact that one of our men had been killed by a sneaky shot, to which he replied that it had not been done by his, but by the neighboring company. "Il y a des cochons aussi chez vous!" (There are pigs in your house too!) he opined, and then a few bullets fired from the our neighboring sector whizzed just past his head, while I tried to take cover as best I could. Meanwhile, we talked a lot more in a way that, I would almost say, expressed a sportsmanlike respect, and at the end we would have gladly exchanged a few memories.

It has always been my ideal in war to regard the enemy as such only in battle, eliminating any feeling of hatred, and to value him as a man according to his temper. I have met many like-minded people among the English officers in this respect.

To get things clear again, we solemnly declared war within three minutes of breaking off negotiations, and after a "Good evening" on his part and an "Au revoir!" on mine, I fired a shot against his shield, despite the regrets of my men, to which he immediately responded with a shot that nearly tore my rifle from my hands.

That was the first time I had been able to get a close look at the "no man's land" between the two trenches, because usually, in that exposed position, one could not even show the edge of one's cap. I saw the skeleton of a Frenchman lying right in front of our barbed wire; white bones glistened through the torn places of his blue uniform.

Shortly after this parley our artillery fired a few shots at the enemy position, whereupon before our eyes four stretchers were carried across the open field without a shot being fired from our side. By the friezes the English wore on their caps we ascertained that that day the Hindostan-Leicestershire regiment was opposite us.

The weather became increasingly bleak toward Christmas; we had to set up pumps in the trenches in order to get some control over the water. We spent Christmas Eve in position. The men, standing in the mud, sang Christmas carols, but the English drowned them out with M.G.'s (machine guns). On Christmas Day we lost a man of the third platoon by a bullet ricochet to the head. Immediately afterwards the English attempted a friendly approach by placing a Christmas tree on their parapet, but it was cut down with a few well-aimed shots by our fierce men, which they, in turn, responded with rifle grenades. Thus our Christmas passed by quite uncomfortably.

On December 28th, I was the commander of the "Altenburg Fortress." On that day one of my best men had his arm torn off by shell fragments. Another was severely wounded in the thigh by one of the many stray bullets that whizzed around our clay fort down in the trench. My faithful August Kettler, on his way to Monchy, from where he was going to fetch my food, was the first of my many boys to fall victim to a shrapnel shot, which knocked him to the ground with a punctured windpipe.

January was another month of even more strenuous work. Each group, using shovels, buckets, and pumps, first removed the mud in the immediate vicinity of its shelter and then, having established solid ground under its feet, sought to establish liaison with neighboring groups. In the forest of Adinfer, the site of our artillery, logging detachments were busy stripping young trees of their branches and splitting them into long logs. The walls of the trenches were rearranged and covered with solid armor. Numerous water drains, wells and drainage ditches were also dug, so that, little by little, we found ourselves in more tolerable living conditions.

On January 28, 1916, a man of my platoon was hit in the body by splinters of a shell that shattered against his shield. On the 30th another received a bullet in the thigh. On February 1st, when the troops arrived for the usual rotation, the access trenches were the object of a very violent shooting. A shell fell, without exploding, right at the feet of Fusilier Junge, who was formerly in charge of my quarters when we were in the 6th Company. It burned, however, sending out a long, intense flame and causing severe burns to the poor fellow, who was immediately sent to the rear.

At about the same time, a non-commissioned officer of the 6th Company, whom I knew very well and whose brother had fallen a few days earlier, was mortally wounded by a ball mine he had found and dismantled. He had unscrewed the fuse and, noticing that the powder burned smoothly, stuck a smoldering cigarette into the opening. The mine, of course, exploded and inflicted over fifty wounds on him. In this and similar ways we had casualties every moment from the recklessness involved in the constant handling of explosives. An uneasy neighbor in this respect was Lieutenant Pook, who occupied a lonely dugout in the tangled trenches behind the left wing. He had hauled a large quantity of huge unexploded bombs there and enjoyed unscrewing and examining the fuses as if they had been pocket watches. I made a big circle around this eerie dwelling every time my way led me past it.

On the night of February 3rd, we had arrived back in Douchy after an exhausting stay in the trenches. The next morning I was sitting in my quarters at Emmich Square, completely immersed in the sweet atmosphere of the first day of rest, in front of a steaming cup of coffee, when suddenly a grenade, the precursor of a massive bombardment, exploded right in front of my door, blowing out a window in my room. In three jumps I reached the cellar, where the other occupants of the house had already arrived with surprising speed. Since the cellar was halfway above ground level and was separated from the garden only by a small wall, they were all trying to squeeze through the narrow, shallow tunnel, the construction of which had begun at that time. My shepherd dog slipped between the tightly packed bodies, driven by his animal instinct, to reach the safest corner. In the distance, at regular intervals, a series of light detonations could be heard, followed by the whistling scream of heavy iron masses that were extinguished in the terrible sound of the explosion all around our little house. Each time an unpleasant air pressure drove through the cellar windows, clods of earth and splinters pattered on the tiled roof, while in the stables the excited horses snorted and kicked. In addition, the dog whined, and a fat musician, at the approach of each whistling sound, would shriek as if a tooth were being pulled.

Finally, the storm having passed, we ventured back out into the open. The village's main street, distraught, swarmed like a gutted anthill. My quarters looked pitiful. Right next to the cellar wall, the ground was completely plowed; some broken fruit trees; and under the vault of the entrance lay, ironically, a long, unexploded shell. The roof was badly punctured. A large splinter had taken half the chimney with it. In the adjoining company office, a few large splinters had pierced the walls and the large closet and shredded almost all the officers' uniforms stored there, to the great annoyance of those affected, of whom I was not one, by the way.

On February 8th, Section C received heavy fire. Early in the morning our own artillery fired a dud into the dugout of my right wing group, which, to the unpleasant surprise of the occupants, smashed in the door and knocked over the stove. A soldier later drew a cartoon of eight men simultaneously pressing over the smoking stove through the shattered door, while the dud winked viciously from a corner. Furthermore, in the afternoon three of our dugouts were shot up, but fortunately only one man was slightly wounded in the knee, since all but the guards had retreated into the tunnels. The following day a man of my platoon was fatally shot in the side by the flanking battery.

On February 25th, we were particularly affected by a death that took away an excellent friend and popular comrade. Shortly before being relieved, I received word in my dugout that the war volunteer K. had just fallen in the tunnel next door. I went there and found, as so often before, a serious group standing around the motionless figure lying with clenched fists on blood-soaked snow, staring with glassy eyes toward the sky. Another victim of the flanking battery! K. had been in the trench at the first shots and immediately jumped into the tunnel. A large splinter from a shell striking the trench wall opposite the entrance whizzed into the entrance of the tunnel and hit him in the back of the head, just when he thought he was safe. He died a quick, unexpected death.

The flanking battery was very active these days. About every hour it fired a single, surprising salvo, the explosive pieces of which swept the trench completely. In six days, from February 3rd to February 8th, it cost us three dead, three seriously wounded and four lightly wounded. Despite the fact that it had to be at most one hundred and fifty meters from us on a hillside on our left flank, it was impossible for our artillery to silence it. Our only means of lessening their effectiveness was to increase and raise our shoulder defenses in order to limit their range to small pieces of trench.

By early March, we had the roughest dirt behind us. The weather became dry, and the trench was neatly boarded up, so that we had a few leisurely free hours more often. Every evening I sat in the dugout in front of my little desk and read or chatted when I had visitors. We were four officers with the company commander and had a very comradely get-together. Every day in the dugout of one or the other we drank coffee or sat down for dinner, often over one or more bottles, smoked, played cards, and carried on a Lansquenets-like conversation. These cozy dugout hours outweigh in memory the many days of blood, dirt and labor. They were also only possible during this long and relatively quiet period of positioning, where we had firmly settled into each other and adopted almost peacetime habits. Our main pride was our activity as builders, not excessively hindered by the Commands of the rear. In restless work, one thirty-step tunnel after the other was driven into the loamy clay soil and connected by cross tunnels, so that we could comfortably reach six meters below ground from the right to the left wing of our position. My favorite work was a sixty-meter-long corridor from me to the company commander's dugout, which had ammunition chambers and living quarters on the right and left. This facility was invaluable during the subsequent fighting.

When we met in the trench after our morning coffee (one even got the newspaper upstairs almost regularly), freshly washed, folding tape measure in hand, we compared the progress of our sections while the conversation turned to cleat frames, dugout patterns, work schedules and similar things. I always felt a pleasant sensation in the evening when I laid down on my bunk, knowing that I had lived up to the expectations of home in my place by putting all my energy into the defense of my two hundred meters of trench and the welfare of my sixty men.

On March 14th, a direct hit of a fifteen-centimeter shell struck our neighboring right section, killing three men and seriously wounding three others. On the 18th, the sentry in front of my dugout received a shell fragment which tore into his cheek and sliced off the tip of one of his ears. On the 19th, a man on the left wing was severely wounded by a shot in the head. On the 23rd, Fusilier L. fell to the right of my dugout, shot in the head. That same evening a sentry reported to me that an enemy patrol was in the wire entanglement. I left the trench with some men, but couldn't find anything.

On April 7th, a man on the right wing was wounded in the head by fragments of a shrapnel bullet. This type of wound was very common in our area as a result of the English ammunition which shatters at the slightest impact. In the afternoon the area around my dugout was pelted with heavy shells for hours. My light well window was shattered for the umpteenth time, and with each detonation a hail of hard clay flew through the opening without, however, being able to disturb us while we were drinking coffee.

Afterwards we had a formal duel with a daredevil Englishman, whose head peered over the edge of a trench not more than a hundred yards away, and who fired a series of hair-trigger shots at our embrasure. I returned fire with a few, but immediately a well-aimed bullet struck the edge of our embrasure, splashing our eyes full of sand and wounding me insignificantly in the neck with a small splinter. However, we did not let up by popping up, taking a quick aim, and disappearing again. Immediately afterwards a bullet exploded on Fusilier Storch's rifle, whose face, hit by at least ten splinters, was bleeding in all places. The next shot tore a piece out of the edge of our embrasure; another shattered the mirror with which we were observing, but we had the satisfaction of seeing our adversary disappear without a trace after a few bullets struck precisely on the clay bank in front of his face. Immediately after that, with three rounds of K ammunition, I shot down the protective shield behind which this rabid fellow had repeatedly appeared.

On April 9th, two English planes repeatedly flew close over our position. The entire trench crew rushed out of the dugouts and opened a furious fire. I was saying to Lieutenant Sievers, who was standing next to me, "As long as the flanking battery doesn't become alert!" when steel fragments flew past our ears, so we both jumped into the nearest tunnel. Sievers was standing in front of the entrance, I advised him to get further in, as he did a splinter as wide as his hand, still steaming, landed right in front of his feet. Immediately after that we received several more shrapnel mines, which exploded over our heads. One man was hit in the armpit by a splinter the size of a pinhead, which was quite painful despite its smallness. I replied with some rifle grenades, for it was the tacit agreement of the infantry to confine themselves to the rifle. The use of explosives was reciprocated in all circumstances at a ratio of at least 2:1. Unfortunately, the enemy usually had such ample ammunition that we ran out of breath first.

After this scare we downed some bottles of red wine in Sievers' dugout, which suddenly put me in such a mood that I walked back to my domicile over cover despite the bright moonlight. Soon I lost my direction, got into a huge crater and heard the English working in the nearby enemy trench. Having been greatly disturbed by two hand grenades, I hastily retreated into our trench, still falling into the erect spike of one of our beautiful trammels consisting of four sharpened iron spikes. These days there was a lot of activity in front of the wire, which sometimes had a certain bloody humor. For example, one of our patrolmen was shot by his own men because he stuttered and couldn't get the password out fast enough. Another time, one of our soldiers, who had been drinking until midnight in the kitchen of Monchy, climbed over the parapet and started 'firing at will' against his own trench. Luckily, he had missed. He was pulled in and soundly beaten.

VI

Prelude to the Battle of the Somme

IN the middle of April of 1916, I was ordered to Croisilles, a small town behind the divisional front, for an officer training course under the personal direction of the division commander, Major General Sontag. Theoretical and practical instruction was given in a whole range of military subjects. The tactical rides under Major von Jarotzky were particularly captivating. Frequent excursions and tours of the rear facilities, most of which had been built out of the ground, gave us, who were accustomed to look over our shoulders at everything that was behind the first trench, an idea of the immense amount of work that was done in the rear of the fighting troops. Thus we visited the slaughterhouse, the provisions depot and the gun repair station at Boyelles, the sawmill and the pioneer park in the Bourlon forest, the dairy, the pig farm and the carcass processing station at Inchy, the airfield and the bakery in Quéant. On Sundays we went to the nearby towns of Cambrai, Douai and Valenciennes "to see women in hats again."

On June 16th, we were released back to the troops by the General with a little speech from which we learned that a major enemy offensive was preparing on the Western Front, the left wing of which would be approximately opposite our position.

That something must be in the air became clear to us even after we returned to the regiment, for our comrades told us of the increasing restlessness of the enemy. The British had twice undertaken a violent patrol against Section C, but without success. We had retaliated by a heavily prepared attack by three officer patrols on the so-called Grabendreieck and had taken quite a number of prisoners. During my absence Lieutenant Wetje had been wounded in the arm by a shrapnel bullet, but immediately after my arrival he took over the command of the company again. My dugout had also changed in the meantime; it had become smaller by half as a result of a hit.

On June 20th, I got the order to listen in front of the enemy trench to see if the enemy was busy with mining work and climbed with Ensign Wohlgemut, Fusilier Schmidt and Fusilier Parthenfelder over our own, rather high wire entanglement. We proceeded stooping the first distance and then crawled side by side across the densely overgrown vegetation. Tertian memories of Karl May came to my mind as I slid on my belly through dewy grass and thistle thickets, anxiously trying to avoid any rustling, since fifty meters in front of us the English trench rose as a black line out of the semi-darkness. The bullets of a distant machine gun clapped down almost vertically around us; every now and then a flare went up to cast its cold light on the inhospitable patch of earth.

At one point, a lively rustling sound was heard behind us, two shadows scurried between the trenches. While we were getting ready to rush at them, they had already disappeared without a trace. Immediately after, a thunderous explosion of two hand grenades in the English trench revealed that it was our own people that had crossed our path. We crept forward slowly.

Suddenly the ensign's hand tightened around my arm: "Watch out on the right, very close, quietly, quietly!" Immediately, ten meters to our right, I heard multiple rustling sounds in the grass. With the lightning-quick logical acuity one develops in such situations, I overlooked it. We had been crawling along the enemy wire all this time, the English had heard us and was now coming out of their trench to investigate the foreland.

Such moments are unforgettable when creeping at night. Eye and ear are strained to the utmost, the approaching rustling of foreign feet in the high grass assumes a strange, ominous strength—it fills one almost completely. The breath comes in jerks; one must force oneself to muffle the gasping contractions. With a small, metallic snap, the safety of the pistol springs back; a sound that goes through your nerves like a knife. Teeth clenched on the fuse of a hand grenade. The collision must be short and murderous. One trembles under two powerful sensations: the heightened excitement of the hunter and the fear of the game. You are a world apart, sucked in by the dark, terrifying atmosphere that hangs over the desolate terrain.

A row of blurred figures appeared close beside us, whispers wafted over. We turned our heads toward them; I heard the Bavarian Parthenfelder bite the blade of his dagger.

They came a few more steps toward us, but then started working on the wire without noticing us. We crawled back very slowly, always keeping an eye on them. Death, who had already been standing in lofty expectation between the parties, slipped away sullenly. After some time we rose and walked upright until we arrived safely in our section.

The good outcome of this excursion inspired us to the thought of taking a prisoner, and we decided to set off again the next evening. In the afternoon, I had just laid down to rest when I was startled awake by a thunder-like crash near my dugout. The English sent over ball mines, which, despite the low firing noise, were of such severity that their splinters cut the tree-thick boarding piles smoothly. Cursing, I climbed down from my bunk and went into the trench. I saw one of the black stalked grenades begin its trajectory from the enemy trench, so I rushed to the next tunnel with the cry: "Grenade left!" Over the next few weeks, we were so abundantly hit with grenades and mines of all sizes and types that we made it a habit to always keep one eye on the air and the other on the nearest tunnel entrance as we made our way through the trench.

So that night I crept around again with three companions between the trenches. We crawled on the tips of our feet and elbows until we were close to the English obstacle and hid there behind single tufts of grass. After some time several Englishmen appeared, dragging a roll of wire. They stopped close in front of us, set the roll down, snipped at it with wire cutters, and talked in whispers. We sidled up to each other and carried on a hasty conversation in hushed tones, "Throw a hand grenade between them and then jump on him!" "Gee, but that's four men!" "There he goes, scared again." "Don't talk nonsense." "Quiet, quiet!" My warning came too late; when I looked up, the Englishmen were just crawling like lizards under their wire and disappearing into the trench. Now the mood did get a little sultry. The thought: "They'll be bringing a machine gun into position in a moment" caused a sour taste in my mouth. The others had similar fears. We slid backward on our bellies with a great clatter of weapons. In the English trench it became lively. Pitter-patter, whispering, running back and forth. Pschschscht . . . a flare. All around, it was as bright as day, while we struggled to hide our heads in tufts of grass. Another flare. Awkward moments. You want to disappear into the earth and be in any other place than ten meters from the enemy trench. Another one. Bang! Bang! The unmistakable sharp, stunning bang of a few rifle shots fired at close range. "Oha! We're spotted!"

Without further consideration, we shouted to each other to run for our lives. We jumped up and raced toward our position where the gun fire was now streaming out. After a few sentences I stumbled and fell into a small, very shallow crater, while the three others, thinking I was done for, rushed past me. I pressed myself hard against the ground, pulled my head and legs in, and let the bullets sweep over me through the tall grass. I was made even more uncomfortable with the glowing magnesium lumps coming down from the falling flares, some of which burned right next to me. Gradually the shooting became weaker, and after another quarter of an hour I left my place of refuge, first slowly, then as fast as possible. Since the moon had set in the meantime, I soon lost all orientation and knew neither where the English nor the German side was. Not even the characteristic ruin of the Monchy mill stood out from the horizon. Every now and then a projectile came flying through the area from one side or the other at a frightening speed. I decided to lay down in the grass and just wait for dawn. Suddenly a few whispers came from close by me. I got into firing position again and, as a cautious man, first gave a series of natural sounds, from which it was impossible to tell whether I was an Englishman or a German. I was about to answer the first English response with a hand grenade when, to my delight, it turned out that it was actually my men in front of me, who were just unbuckling the paddock to carry me back. We sat together in the crater for a while longer, rejoicing in our being reunited. Then we headed back to our trench, which we reached after three hours of absence.

In the morning I had digging duty again at 5 o'clock. In the section of the first platoon, I found Sergeant H. in front of his dugout. I wondered why I was seeing him at such an early hour—he told me that he was at the dugout waiting for a big rat, which robbed him of his night's sleep. As he was talking, he kept looking at his ridiculously small shelter, which he had named the "Chicken Coop."

As we stood side by side, we heard a muffled bang, which, however, didn't mean anything special. H., who had almost been killed by a large spherical bomb the day before and was therefore very nervous, darted like lightning to the nearest tunnel entrance, slid down the first fifteen steps while sitting and used the last fifteen to do a triple somersault. I stood at the top of the entrance, completely forgetting about the sound, and fell with laughter when I heard this painful interruption of a rat hunt lamented by the poor man while sensitively rubbing various parts of his body. The unlucky fellow also confessed to me that he had just sat for supper yesterday when the bomb arrived, making a waste of all of his food. And he ended up tumbling down the same stairs that he did today.

After this exhilarating episode I went to my dugout, but I wasn't going to get a refreshing nap today either. From early morning on, our trench was pelted with mortars at ever shorter intervals. Around noon, the situation became too much for me. Together with some men I prepared our Lanz mortar and took the enemy trenches under fire, a somewhat feeble response to the heavy projectiles with which we were abundantly showered. Sweating, we squatted on the clay of a small trench, baked hot by the June sun, and sent shell after shell across. Since the English did not seem to notice our efforts at all, I went with Lieutenant Wetje to the telephone, where, after careful consideration, we let the following distress call ring out: "Helene is spitting in our trench, lots of thick clumps, we need potatoes, big and small!" This gibberish was used in order not to betray anything to the enemy who might be listening in; soon Lieutenant Deichmann gave us the comforting answer that the fat sergeant with the tight mustache and some small boys would come forward immediately, and right after that our first hundred-kilogram shell plunged into the enemy trench with an unbelievable crash, followed by several volleys of field artillery; we had peace for the rest of the day.

At noon the next day, the dance began in a much sharper manner. At the first shots, I went through my underground passage into the second trench and from there into the barrel trench where we had set up our Lanz mortar. We opened fire in such a way that we fired a Lanz mortar at every incoming shell. After we had exchanged about forty shells, the enemy gunner seemed to turn on us personally. Soon some shells struck to our right, others to our left, unable to interrupt our activity until one came straight at us. We fired one more mortar and then ran away as fast as we could. I had just entered a muddy, barbed wire-strewn trench when the monster exploded close behind me. The tremendous air pressure threw me over a bundle of barbed wire into a crater filled with greenish mud, while at the same time a shower of hard lumps of clay rattled down upon me. Half stunned and badly battered, I rose. My pants and boots were torn by the barbed wire, my face, hands and uniform were covered with thick clay, and my knee was bleeding from a long scrape. Quite worn out, I crept through the trench to my dugout to rest.

Otherwise, the enemy bombs had not done much damage. The trench had been destroyed in some places, our Lanz Mortar had been shattered to pieces, and the "Chicken Coop" had received a direct hit. The unfortunate owner had already been sitting at the bottom of the tunnel, otherwise he probably would have taken his third fall down the stairs on this occasion.

The storm continued uninterruptedly all afternoon and increased to a drumfire in the evening hours by a myriad of cylindrical projectiles. Our men called these cylindrical bombs the "laundry basket bombs" because it sometimes seemed as if they were poured from the sky from upturned baskets.

We sat in the tunnel entrances with eager anticipation, ready to greet each arrival with rifle and hand grenade, but the fire died down again after half an hour. During the night we had to endure two more fire raids, during which our sentries remained steadfastly on the lookout in their positions. As soon as the fire subsided, many rising flares illuminated the defenders rushing out of their tunnels, and a furious fire convinced the enemy of the indomitable determination of the Hanoverian fusiliers.

Despite the insane fire, we only lost one man, whose skull was crushed by a bomb that exploded against his protective shield. Another was wounded in the back.

Also, during the day, which replaced this restless night, numerous dense shootings prepared us for an imminent attack. During this time our trench was turned upside down and made almost impassable by the shattered timbers of the boarding, also a number of dugouts were completely crushed.

We all decided to stay awake during the coming night and agreed that anyone who did not shout out his name at the first warning would be shot down immediately. Each officer had loaded his flare gun with a red flare so that the artillery could be notified immediately.

The night became even more awesome than the previous one. At a quarter past two a fire attack surpassed everything that we had seen up to that point. A hail of heavy shells swept all around my dugout. We stood in full armor on the stairs of the tunnel; the light from the small candle stumps gleamed many times on the wet, moldy walls. Blue smoke poured through the entrances, earth crumbled from the ceiling. Boom! "Golly!" "Match, match!" "Get everything ready!" My heart was beating up to my neck. Nervous hands loosened the capsules of the hand grenades. "That was the last one!" "Let's go!" As we rushed for the exit, another bomb went off with delayed burst, flinging us back again with its air pressure. Nevertheless, while the last iron birds were still hurtling down, all the post stands were already occupied by the valiant crew. A rapid fire surged out, and flares shone midday brightness on the foreland, which was covered with thick clouds of smoke.

As soon as the fire started to die down, we suffered another loss. Fusilier N. suddenly fell from his post and rolled tumbling down the stairs into the midst of his comrades gathered below. When we examined the unearthly arrival, we found a small wound on his forehead and a bleeding hole above his right nipple. It remained unclear whether the wound or the precipitous fall had brought about his death.

At the end of this night of terror we were relieved by the 6th Company. With that peculiar mood of discontent which a landscape shining in the morning sun exerts on exhausted, overtired nerves, we moved through the trenches to Monchy and from there to the second position stretching in front of the edge of the Adinfer forest, from where we had a magnificent view of the prelude to the battle of the Somme. The frontal sections to our left were shrouded in clouds of white and black smoke, one heavy impact exploded tower-high next to the other; above them, the short flashes of bursting shrapnel crackled by the hundreds.

In that evening, when all we wanted to do was sleep, we were ordered to load heavy mines at Monchy and had to wait all night in vain for some stuck wagon, while the English made various, fortunately unsuccessful, attempts on our lives with machine gun fire and shrapnel sweeping down the road.

That night, the enemy gave me an example of the awesome precision of his observation. In the second position, about two thousand yards from the enemy, a mound of clay was piled up in front of an ammunition tunnel under construction. The English drew from this the unfortunately correct conclusion that this mound would be warped during the night and fired a hail of shrapnel at it, by which they severely wounded three of our men.

In the morning, I was jolted out of sleep again by another order, this time to lead my platoon to Section C to reinforce the trench. I was then ordered to take my platoon to the next section. My groups were distributed within the 6th Company. I went back to the Adinfer forest with a few men to put them to work chopping wood. On the way back to the position I stepped into my dugout to rest there for half an hour. But in vain, I was unable to find undisturbed rest these days. I had hardly taken off my boots when I heard our artillery opening a strangely lively fire from the edge of the forest. At the same time my lad Paulicke appeared at the entrance to the tunnel and shouted down: "Gas attack!"

I tore out the gas mask, put on my boots, buckled my belt, ran outside, and there I saw a massive cloud of gas hanging in dense whitish plumes over Monchy and slowly rolling toward Point 124.

Since most of my platoon was in position in front and an attack seemed very likely, there was no time to waste in thinking. I jumped over the second position's obstacle, ran forward and was soon in the middle of the gas cloud. I put my mask on and immediately tore it off. I had been running so hard that I couldn't get enough air through the filter; also, the eye glasses were fogged up and turned completely opaque in no time. Since I felt pricks in my chest, I tried to at least get through the cloud as quickly as possible. Before reaching the edge of the village, I had to pass through a barrage of fire whose impacts, punctuated by numerous clouds of shrapnel, traced a long chain across the desolate fields that were otherwise never entered.

Artillery fire in such open terrain, where one can move freely, has neither the same material force nor the same moral effect as it has on clusters of houses or in the trenches. So in no time at all I had put the line of fire behind me and found myself in Monchy, which was under a tremendous hail of shrapnel. A shower of bullets, shrapnel and shells swept through the branches of the fruit trees in the overgrown gardens and slapped against the crumbling walls of the houses.

In a dugout of the gardens, I found my mates Sievers and Vogel sitting; they had lit a blazing wood fire and were bending over the purifying flame to escape the poisonous effects of the chlorine. I kept them company in this occupation until the fire had died down, and then went forward through trench six. As I strolled very slowly through the trench in my incorrigible phlegm, only fifty meters from the company leader's dugout, I was once again caught in a mad fire attack and, pressed into a small niche, had to endure the storm.

In front, all the men were busy greasing their rifles, which were completely blackened by the gas. An ensign gloomily showed me his new saber, which had lost its beautiful shine and instead had taken on a greenish-black appearance.

Since everything had remained quiet with the enemy, I moved off again with my men. In Monchy we saw a crowd of gas patients sitting in front of the aid station, pressing their hands into their sides, moaning and choking while tears streamed down from their eyes. The affair was by no means harmless, for some of them ended up dying several days later after suffering excruciating pain. We had had to endure a blast of pure chlorine, a combat gas that works by cauterizing and burning the lungs. On the way back, I went to buy something in the commissary of the 2nd Battalion and found the saddened canteen boy there in the midst of a pile of smashed goods. A shell had gone through the ceiling, exploded in the store, and turned his treasures into a strange mixture of jam, spilled canned goods, and soap. He had just drafted an expense sheet of eighty-two marks and fifty-eight pennies with true Prussian precision.

In the evening, my platoon, which until then had been detached in the second position, was pulled forward to the village because of the uncertain battle situation and was ordered to stay in the mine. We set up the numerous niches as campsites and lit a huge fire, the smoke of which we let escape through the well shaft, much to the annoyance of some company cooks who almost suffocated while fetching water. Having received a strong grog, we sat down around the fire on the clay blocks, singing, drinking and smoking.

At midnight, a hellish spectacle went off in the battle arc of Monchy. Dozens of alarm bells rang, hundreds of guns blazed, and green and white flares rose incessantly. Immediately our barrage began, heavy shells cracked and trailing tails of fiery sparks were seen everywhere. A soul dwelt in the tangle of the rubble, the long-drawn cry rang out, "Gas attack!" "Gas attack!"

In the glow of the flares, a whitish wall of gas was seen rolling through the village. Since a strong smell of chlorine was also noticeable in the mine, we lit large straw fires in front of the entrances, whose mordant smoke almost drove us out of our place of refuge and forced us to purify the air by waving coats and tent canvases.

The next morning we marveled at the horrible effects of the gas attack in the village. A large part of all the plants had withered, snails and moles laid dead all around, and the horses of the dispatch riders housed in Monchy had water running out of their mouths and eyes. The bullets and shell fragments scattered everywhere were covered with a beautiful green patina. Even in Douchy, which was far behind, the gas cloud had left its traces. The civilians, who were getting spooked, gathered in front of Lieutenant Colonel von Oppen's quarters and demanded gas masks. They were put on trucks and transported to villages further back.

We spent the next night in the mine again; in the evening I received news that coffee was to be received at a quarter past four a.m., since an English defector had testified that there would be an attack at 5 o'clock. Really, I had hardly been disturbed from my sleep in the morning by the returning coffee-haulers when the call "Gas attack!" which was no longer strange to us, rang out. Outside there was a sweet phosgene smell in the air, and in the Monchy arc a strong drum fire was raging, but it soon died down.

A refreshing morning followed this uneasy hour. From trench six, Lieutenant Brecht stepped out onto the village street, a bloody bandage around his hand, accompanied by a man with a mounted bayonet and a captured Englishman. He was received triumphantly at the West Command Quarters and related the following:

The English had set off clouds of gas and smoke at 5 o'clock and then heavily pounded the trench. Our people, as usual, had jumped from cover while still under fire, suffering over thirty casualties. Then, hidden in clouds of smoke, two strong English patrols had appeared, one of which had entered the trench and taken a wounded NCO. The other had already been decimated in front of the wire entanglement.

An Englishman, isolated, had managed to get through, but Brecht, who had been a planter in America before the war, had grabbed him by the throat and shouted, "Come here, you son of a bitch!" This sole survivor was served a glass of wine and looked with half startled, half astonished eyes at the village street, which had just been deserted and was now crawling with men fetching food, carrying sick people, order bearers and the curious.

A long procession of stretchers arrived at the dressing station. From south Monchy came a great many more wounded because the enemy had managed to infiltrate, albeit briefly, as far as Sector E. About fifty stretchers, on which moaning people with white, blood-soaked bandages laid, were lined up under some corrugated metal canopies, where a doctor was performing his duties.

A young fellow, with his blue lips shining as a bad omen from his snow-white face, stammered, "I'm too heavy . . . I'm not going to make it . . . I—must—die." A fat medical sergeant looked at him pityingly and murmured several times a consoling, "Come on, come on, comrade!"

Although the English had prepared this small attack, which was mainly intended to tie up our forces for the advantage of the Somme offensive, by numerous bomb raids and gas clouds, only one loss, in addition to a wounded prisoner that fell into their hands, while they left numerous dead in front of our wire. Our losses, however, were also considerable; the regiment lost over forty men that morning, including three officers.

The next day, in the afternoon, we finally headed back again to our dear Douchy for a few days. That same evening we celebrated the happy outcome of the battle with a few well deserved bottles.

On July 1st, we were given the sad task of burying some of our dead in our cemetery. Thirty-nine crude wooden coffins were lowered into the pit after a moving speech by pastor Philippi, during which people cried like children. The priest spoke over the text: "You have fought a good fight," and began with the words: "Gibraltar, this is your symbol and truth, you have resisted like the rock resists the surf!"

In this poignant hour, the high ethical value of our solemn acts became clear to me. Often we had to leave ten times the number of comrades on some battlefield and were not so deeply gripped by the loss as here in front of the open graves.

During these days I came to appreciate the men with whom I was to spend three more years fighting. In the whole army you will not find a man who does his duty as reliably, simply and without phrase as the Lower Saxon. When it was necessary to show up: here he stands, and if it must be, here he falls.

On the evening of July 3rd, we moved forward again. It was relatively quiet, but small signs revealed that something was still in the air. At the mill there was faint, incessant knocking and hammering. Often we caught suspicious long-distance conversations concerning gas cylinders and blasting, addressed to an English engineer officer on the front line. From dawn until the last glimmer of day, enemy planes delivered a dense air barrage. The average daily trench bombardment was significantly heavier than usual.

Nevertheless, we were relieved on July 12th without having had any unpleasant experiences and remained in reserve at Monchy.

On the evening of the 13th, our dugouts in the gardens were fired upon by a 240 mm caliber naval gun, whose giant shells thundered over in a sharp trajectory and explode with a truly terrifying blast. During the night we were awakened by a gas attack and a lively fire. We sat around the stove in the dugout with our gas masks on, except for Vogel, who couldn't find his mask and ran whining back and forth, while some gleeful fellows pretended to sense an ever stronger smell of gas. I finally gave him my second breathing filter, and he squatted for an hour in despair behind the fiercely smoking stove, holding his nose with a cantankerous face while sucking on the filter.

No attacks were made that night; nevertheless, the silly incident cost the regiment twenty-five dead and many wounded. On the 15th and 17th we had to endure two more gas attacks. On the 17th we were relieved and had to endure two heavy shelling attacks at Douchy. One surprised us during an officers' meeting by Major von Jarotzky in an orchard. Despite the danger, it was a sight of overwhelming comedy to see the company scatter, fall on their noses, squeeze through the hedgerows with incredible speed, and disappear in a flash into all sorts of cover. One of the shells ended up killing an eight-year-old little girl in the garden of my quarters, who was there looking for scraps in a pit.

On July 20th, we moved into position. On the 28th I arranged to go on patrol with Ensign Wohlgemut and Fusiliers Bartels and Birkner. We had no other goal in mind than to roam around a bit between the wires and see what new things no man's land would bring us. In the afternoon the officer relieving me from the 6th Company, Lieutenant Brauns, came to visit me in my dugout and brought several good bottles with him. At a half past 12 o'clock we broke up the meeting; I went into the trench, where my three companions were already standing together in a dark corner. After selecting some dry hand grenades, I climbed over the wire in the most cheerful mood, while Brauns shouted a "Good luck!" to me.

We had crept through the enemy obstacle in a short amount of time. Close in front of it, we discovered a rather strong, well-insulated wire in the high grass. I considered the observation important and instructed Wohlgemut to cut off a piece of it and take it with him. While he was working on it with his cigar scissors for lack of another instrument, there was a clang in the wire directly in front of us; some Englishmen appeared and began to work without noticing our figures pressed into the grass.

Remembering the bad experience of the previous patrol, I breathed almost inaudibly, "Wohlgemut, throw a hand grenade!" "Lieutenant, I think we should let them work a little longer!" "That's a direct order, Ensign!"

The spirit of the Prussian barracks yard did not miss its powerful effect even in this wasteland. With the fatal feeling of a man who has embarked on a very uncertain adventure, I heard the dry crackling of the torn-out fuse next to me and saw Wohlgemut, in order to show himself as little as possible, let the hand grenade roll very flat over the ground. It stopped in the bushes, almost between the Englishmen, who seemed to have noticed nothing. A few moments of supreme suspense passed. "Krrrach!" A flash of lightning illuminated staggering figures. With a roar of attack, "You are prisoners!" we plunged like tigers into the white cloud. A wild scene unwound in a split second. I aimed my gun at a face that stood before me emerging from the darkness like a white mask. A shadow fell backward into the wire entanglement with a nasally yelp. To my left, Wohlgemut fired his pistol, while Fusilier Bartels, in his excitement, blindly hurled a hand grenade between us.

With the first shot the magazine had popped out of my pistol butt without me noticing. I stood screaming in front of an Englishman who, horrified, pressed his back into the barbed wire. I kept pulling my trigger without a shot being fired. It was like a nightmare. It became loud in the trench in front of us. Shouts rang out, a machine gun rattled. We jumped back. I stopped in a crater and pointed my pistol and fired at a shadow following me. This time the empty gun turned out to be good luck, because the shadow was Birkner, whom I had thought to be with us already.

Now we ran at full speed to our own trench. In front of our wire the projectiles were already whizzing by in such a way that I was forced to jump into a water-filled, wire-spun crater. Swinging on barbed wire above the water level, I heard with mixed feelings the bullets roaring over me like a mighty swarm of bees, while shreds of wire and bullet fragments swept into the embankment of the crater. After half an hour, when the fire had calmed down, I worked my way over our obstacle and, greeted joyfully by the men, jumped into the trench. Wohlgemut and Bartels were already there; after another half hour, Birkner also appeared. Everyone rejoiced at the happy outcome and only regretted that the longed-for prisoner had slipped away this time as well. I realized that the experience had gotten on my nerves when I was lying on a cot in the dugout with my teeth chattering, unable to find any sleep despite my exhaustion. The next morning I could hardly walk because of a long barbed wire scrape across one knee and a splinter of the hand grenade thrown by Bartels in the other.

These short, sporty sensations, however, were a good way to steel one's courage and break the monotony of being in the trench.

On August 11th, a black riding horse was running around in the English rear area in front of the village of Berles-au-bois, and was brought down by a Landwehr man with three shots. The English officer, from whom it had escaped, must not have been very amused at the sight. During the night the casing of an infantry bullet flew into the eye of Fusilier S. In the village, too, casualties became more frequent, as the walls, shaved by artillery fire, offered less and less protection from the sheaves of machine gun bullets. We began to cut the village with new trenches and raise the walls in the most dangerous areas.

August 12th was the long-awaited day when I could go on leave for the second time during the war. However, I had hardly warmed up at home when a telegram was sent me: "Return immediately, ask for details at the Cambrai local commandant's office." Three hours later I was on the train. On the way to the station, three girls walked past me in bright clothes, laughing, with tennis rackets under their arms. A radiant farewell to life, which I had to think about for a long time outside.

On the 21st I was back in the familiar area, whose streets were teeming with troops due to the departure of the 3rd Division and the arrival of a new one. The 1st Battalion was in the village of Ecoust-Saint-Mein, which we stormed again two years later, where I spent the night with eight other officers in the attic of an empty house.

In the evening we sat awake for a long time and, lacking anything stronger, drank the coffee brewed for us by two French women in the house next door. We knew that this time it was going to be a battle the likes of which world history had never seen. Soon the excited conversation swelled to a din that would have delighted old lansquenets or Frederician grenadiers. After a few days, only a few participants of this merry round table were still alive.

VII

Guillemont

ON August 23, 1916, we were loaded into trucks and drove to Le Mesnil. Although we had already learned that we were to be deployed in the then focal point of the battle of the Somme, the village of Guillemont, the mood was excellent. Jokes flew from one car to another amid general laughter. From Le Mesnil, after dark, we marched to Sailly-Saillisel, where the battalion laid down its knapsacks and prepared assault packs in a large meadow. In front of us an artillery barrage of an unbelievable strength rolled and thundered, a thousand lightning flashes enveloped the western horizon in a glowing sea of flames. Wounded men with pale, sunken faces were constantly dragging themselves back, often abruptly pushed into the trench by rattling artillery.

A man in a steel helmet instructed me to lead my platoon to the famous town of Combles, where we were to remain in reserve for the time being. Sitting next to him in the trench, I naturally asked eagerly about the conditions in the position and heard a monotonous tale of squatting for days in shell craters without communication or avenues of approach, of incessant attacks, of fields of corpses and insane thirst, of the wounded languishing and more. The immobile face, half framed by the steel helmet, and the monotonous voice, accompanied by the noise of the front, gave the impression of a sinister seriousness. One could tell that the man had tasted every horror to the point of despair and then learned to despise it. Nothing seemed to remain but a great and manly indifference.

"If you fall, you stay down. No one can help. No one knows if they will come back alive. Every day they attack, but they can't get through. Everyone knows that it is a matter of life and death."

One can go into battle with a man like that.

We walked along a wide road, which stretched across the dark terrain in the moonlight like a white ribbon, towards the thunder of the cannons, whose devouring roar became more and more immense. Leave all hope behind! Soon the first shells struck to the right and left of our path. The conversations became quieter and finally died down completely. Everyone listened with that strange tension that concentrates all feeling and thinking on the ear, to the drawn howling of the shells. Especially the passing of Frégicourt-Ferme, a small group of farm houses in front of the Combles cemetery, which was under constant fire, was a test on the nerves.

Combles was, as far as we could observe in the darkness, completely shot up. Large quantities of wood, among the debris, as well as household utensils, strewn all over the path, inferred that the destruction must have happened very recently. After climbing over numerous piles of rubble, accelerated by a series of shrapnel bursts, we reached our quarters, a large house riddled with holes, which I and three groups chose as their residence, while my other two groups occupied the cellar of a ruin opposite ours.

At 4 o'clock we were awakened from our camp, made up of pieces of beds from the house, to receive the delivery of steel helmets. On this occasion, we found a sack full of coffee beans in a cellar niche, a discovery that resulted in an eager coffee brewing session.

After I had had breakfast, I decided to take a little look around the town. In a few days, the impact of heavy artillery had transformed a small peaceful town into a scene of horror. Entire houses had been collapsed by a shell or torn apart in the middle, so that the rooms and their furnishings floated like theater sets above the chaos. The sweet smell of corpses emanated from many ruins, for the initial attack had buried scores of civilians under the rubble of their homes. At the front door of one house laid a dead little girl in a pool of blood.

One place that was heavily shelled was the square in front of the destroyed church opposite the entrance to the catacombs, an ancient cavernous passage with blasted-in niches where, huddled together, almost all the staffs of the fighting troops lived. It was said that when the shelling began, the civilians had used pickaxes to break through the walled entrance, which they had concealed from the Germans throughout the occupation.

The streets consisted only of narrow trails that wound in serpentine lines through and over massive mounds of beams and masonry. In rumpled gardens, a myriad of fruits and vegetables decayed.

After lunch, which we had cooked for ourselves in the kitchen from the abundant reserve supplies and which was naturally concluded by a strong coffee, I laid down in an armchair upstairs. From letters lying around I saw that the house belonged to the brewery owner Lesage. In the rooms I found gutted closets and dressers, an overturned dressing table, a sewing machine and a baby carriage. Torn pictures and shattered mirrors hung on the walls. On the floor, torn out drawers, linen, corsets, books, newspapers, bedside tables, broken glass, bottles, music books, chair legs, skirts, coats, lamps, curtains, shutters, doors torn off their hinges, lace, photographs, oil paintings, albums, smashed boxes, ladies' hats, flower pots, and tattered wallpaper were tangled together in a meter-high mess.

Through the demolished shutters one could see a desolate square plowed by shells and covered by the branches of tattered lime trees. This complex of impressions was further obscured by the incessant artillery fire that raged all around the place. Every now and then the gigantic impact of a 380 mm shell would resound over the din. Clouds of shrapnel then swept through Combles, slapping against the branches of the trees or hitting the few houses still standing, causing their shingles to slide off.

In the course of the afternoon the fire swelled to such a strength that only the feeling of a tremendous roar remained, in which every single sound was swallowed up. From 7 o'clock on, the square and the surrounding houses were pelted with 150 mm shells at half-minute intervals. There were many duds among them, which nevertheless still made the houses sway. We sat in our basement on silk-covered armchairs around a table during the whole time, resting our heads in our hands and counting the time between each impact. The witticisms became rarer and rarer, and at last the strain of nerves silenced even the most audacious. At 8 o'clock the outhouse collapsed after two direct hits.

From 9 to 10 o'clock the fire took on an insane force. The earth swayed, the sky seemed like a seething giant cauldron.

Hundreds of heavy batteries thundered into and around Combles, countless shells crossed overhead howling and hissing. Everything was shrouded in dense smoke, illuminated ominously by colorful flares. With the most severe headaches and earaches, we could only communicate by shouting incomplete words. The ability of logical thinking and the feeling of gravity seemed to be suspended. One had the sensation of the inescapable and absolutely necessary, as if facing an outbreak of the elements. A sergeant of the third platoon became raving mad.

At 10 o'clock, this carnival of hell gradually calmed down and transformed into a quiet drumfire, in which, however, it was still not possible to distinguish the detached shots from each other.

At 11 o'clock an orderly came and brought orders to lead the platoons to the church square. We then united with the other two platoons to march into position. In order to bring rations to the front, another platoon, led by Lieutenant Sievers, had been sent out. The remaining men came around us while we gathered, with short calls, in that dangerous place, and loaded us with the food that was still abundant at that time. Sievers forced a cooking pot full of butter on me, squeezed my hand in farewell and wished us good luck.

Then we marched off in line, one behind the other. Everyone had orders to keep behind the person in front of him. As soon as we left the village, our leader realized that he had lost his way. We were forced to turn back under heavy shrapnel fire. Then we went, mostly at a running pace, along a white band laid out for orientation, shot into small pieces, over open fields. We often had to stop when the guide had lost the direction, and always in the worst places. It was forbidden to lie down in order to maintain the connection.

Nevertheless, the first and third trains suddenly disappeared. Forward! In a heavily shelled trench the groups piled up. Lie down! A sickeningly intrusive smell informed us that this passage had already claimed many victims. After a life-threatening run, we reached a second trench, which contained the dugout of the combat troop commander (K. T. K.), lost our way and turned back in the agonizing throng of nervous and excited men. No more than five meters from Lieutenant Vogel and myself, a medium sized shell struck the rear embankment with a dull thud, pelting us with huge clods of earth, while shivers of death slid down our spines. At last the guide found his way again through the landmark of a conspicuous pile of corpses.

Go on! Go on! Many men collapsed on our way; with outrageous threats we forced them to pump the last bit of strength from their exhausted bodies. Wounded men hit the craters on the right and left with unheeded cries for help. On we went, eyes fixed on the man in front, through a knee-deep trench formed by a chain of huge craters, where one dead man laid next to another. Reluctantly, my foot stepped on the soft, yielding corpses. The wounded who fell along the way were equally destined to be trampled under the boots of those rushing onwards.

And always that sweet smell! Even my combat orderly, little Schmidt, companion on many dangerous patrols, was beginning to stagger. I snatched the rifle from his hand, the good boy, even at that moment, tried to resist out of politeness.

We finally reached the front line, which was occupied by men huddled close together in the holes, whose toneless voices trembled with joy when they learned that their relief had arrived. A Bavarian sergeant, with a few words, handed me the section and a flare gun.

My platoon's section formed the right wing of the regimental position and consisted of a shallow, trough-like trench a few hundred meters to the left of Guillemont and a little closer to the right of the Bois de Trônes. From the neighboring force on the right, 76th Infantry Regiment, we were separated by an unoccupied space five hundred meters wide, in which no one could stay because of the exceedingly intense fire concentrated there.

The Bavarian sergeant had suddenly disappeared out of sight, and I was standing there all alone, my flare gun in my hand, in the middle of an eerie crater-ridden terrain, which was shrouded in an even more ominous and mysterious appearance by white clouds of fog stagnating on the ground. Behind me, a persistent, unpleasant sound rang out; I determined with strange objectivity that it was coming from a giant, decomposing corpse.

Since it was not even clear to me where the enemy might approximately be, I went to my men and advised them to be prepared for the worst. We all stayed awake; I spent the night with my lad and my two battle orderlies in a foxhole of perhaps one cubic meter capacity.

As the morning dawned, the strange surroundings gradually unveiled themselves to the curious eyes. The path appeared only as a series of huge craters filled with pieces of uniform, weapons and dead bodies; the surrounding terrain was, as far as the eye could see, completely devastated by heavy shells. Not a single pathetic blade of grass was visible to the searching eye. The rumpled battlefield was gruesome. Among the living defenders laid the dead. Digging holes for cover, we noticed that bodies were piled in layers on top of each other. One company after the other was densely packed in the barrage, waiting to be annihilated. Then the bodies were buried by the masses of earth raised by shells, and the next company had taken the place of the fallen.

The trench and the terrain behind it was full of Germans, the terrain in front of it was full of English. Arms, legs and heads were sticking out of the embankments; in front of our holes in the ground laid torn-off limbs and dead bodies, over some of which, to escape the constant sight of the disfigured faces, coats or canvas had been thrown. Despite the heat, no one thought to cover the bodies with earth.

The village of Guillemont differed from the rest of the terrain only in that the craters were of a whiter color as a result of the stones of the houses being crushed into dust. In front of us was the station of Guillemont, crumpled like a child's toy, and further back the forest of Delville, reduced to chips.

The day had hardly dawned when a low-flying Englishman swooped down and circled us like a carrion bird, while we fled into our holes and huddled there. The sharp eye of the observer must have spotted us anyway, because soon low, prolonged siren sounds were heard from above at short intervals. After a short time, a battery seemed to have picked up the signals. One heavy flat-bore shell after another hurtled in with incredible force. We crouched idly in our places of refuge, occasionally lighting a cigar and tossing it away again, wary of being buried at any moment. Schmidt's coat sleeve was torn by a large piece of shrapnel.

Right at the third barrage the inhabitant of the hole in the ground next to us was buried by a tremendous impact. We immediately dug him out again; nevertheless, he was exhausted to death by the pressure of the earth masses, his face sunken and resembling a skull. It was Fusilier Simon. He had become wise due to the impact, because when men moved out of their cover in the course of the day, one heard his scolding voice and saw his fist shake menacingly from an opening of his tarp-covered foxhole.

At 3 o'clock in the afternoon, my men stationed at the posts to my left stated that they could no longer hold on because their fox-holes have been completely flattened by shells. I had to use all of my ruthlessness to get them back in their places.

Shortly before 10 o'clock in the evening a firestorm started on the left wing of the regiment, which after twenty minutes also spread to us. After a short time we were completely enveloped in smoke and dust, but most of the impacts were close in front of or behind the trench. With the hurricane roaring around us, I inspected the section held by my platoon. The men stood as motionless as statues, rifle in hand, on the front slope of the trench, staring into the foreland. Now and then in the glow of a flare I saw a shiny row of steel helmets, rifle next to rifle, and was filled with the proud feeling of commanding a handful of men who might be crushed but could not be defeated. At such moments, the human spirit triumphs over the most formidable expressions of matter, the frail body, steeled by will, is able to confront the most terrible storms.

In the left neighboring platoon, Sergeant H., the unfortunate Pied Piper of Monchy, meant to fire a white flare, but made a mistake and instead shot up a red flare, signaling a barrage, hissing towards the sky, which relayed from both sides. In an instant, our artillery began to fire in such a way that it was a joy. One shell after another came howling down high from the skies and shattered into splinters and sparks in the foreland. A mixture of dust, suffocating gases and the stench of corpses thrown into the air rose from the craters. After this orgy of destruction, the fire returned to baseline, which it maintained throughout the night and the next day. The excited blunder of a single man had set off the entire mighty war machine. H. was and remained an unlucky man; that same night, while loading his flare gun, he shot himself in the boot and had to be carried to the medic with severe burns.

It rained heavily the next day, which was not unwelcome to us, since the parched feeling in the roof of our mouths was not so tormenting after the dust had disappeared, and the large blue-black flies, which had collected in huge clusters in the sunny places, were driven away. I sat on the ground in front of my foxhole for most of the day, smoking and eating with a good appetite despite the environment.

The next morning Fusilier Knicke of my platoon took a rifle shot to the chest, which also grazed his spinal cord, paralyzing his legs. I went to check on him and found him lying in a hole in the ground in a very restrained manner. He was dragged through the artillery fire in the evening, breaking another leg by the frequent jumping for cover by the men carrying him. He died at the dressing station.

In the afternoon, a man from my platoon called me and had me aim my binoculars over the torn off leg of an Englishman to the Guillemont station. I saw hundreds of Englishmen rushing forward through a shallow running trench. They were hardly disturbed by the weak gunfire that I immediately directed at them. This sight was indicative of the inequality of means with which we fought. Had we dared to do the same, our divisions would have been shot to pieces within a few minutes. While not one of our tethered observation balloons were to be seen, on the English side more than thirty stood in a clump and watched with wary eyes every movement that appeared in the trampled terrain in order to immediately direct a hail of iron there.

In the evening, a large piece of shrapnel hit me in the stomach; fortunately it was almost at the end of its trajectory and fell to the ground after hitting my belt buckle with a powerful blow. In front of the section of the first platoon, at nightfall, two English food fetchers appeared who had lost their way. Both of them were shot down at point blank range; one ended up with his torso in the trench and his legs sticking up over the parapet. Taking prisoners was undesirable to all the men, for how could they be brought through the barrage zone that they themselves had a hand in?

Around 1 o'clock a.m. I was shaken out of a confused sleep by Schmidt. Nervously, I pulled myself up and reached for the rifle. Our relief had arrived. We handed over what needed to be handed over and left this hellhole as quickly as possible.

We had hardly reached the shallow running trench when the first volley of shrapnel exploded between us. My front man staggered and wanted to lie on his side as a result of a wound on his wrist from which blood was spurting profusely. I grabbed him by the arm, pulled him up in spite of his groans, and handed him over to the first-aid shelter next to the K. T. K.

In both trenches, the action was sharp. We were terribly out of breath. The worst area was a valley into which we ran, and in which shrapnel and light shells pummeled incessantly. Brrruch! Brrruch! The iron whirlwind overturned us, spraying a shower of sparks into the darkness. Huiiiii! Another cluster! I stood with bated breath as I realized, a few fractions of a second earlier, from the increasingly high-pitched howl, that the downward part of a shell's trajectory would end right at my location. Immediately thereafter, a heavy blow shook the ground near my feet, flinging up soft pieces of clay. Fortunately for me, the shell was a dud!

Here was a prime opportunity to assert the officer's influence. Everywhere, detaching and detached squads hurried through the night and fire, some of them completely lost, groaning from excitement and exhaustion; in between, shouts, orders and, in monotonous repetition, the long-drawn-out cries for help in the crater terrain of lost, wounded men resounded. I gave information to the lost as I raced past, pulled men out of shell holes, threatened those who wanted to lie down, kept shouting my name to keep everyone together, and thus miraculously brought my platoon to Combles.

We still had to march from Combles through Sailly and the Ferme du Gouvernement to the forest of Hennois, where we were to make camp. It was only then that our exhaustion became fully apparent. Heads dully turned to the ground, we crept along our road, often pushed to the side by automobiles or columns of ammunition trucks. In a kind of morbid nervousness I was firmly convinced that the passing vehicles drove so closely along the roadside only to annoy us, and I caught myself more than once with my hand on the butt of my revolver.

After the march we still had to pitch our tents, after which we were finally able to throw ourselves on the rock hard ground. During our stay in this forest camp we received tremendous downpours. The straw in the tents began to rot, and many people fell ill. The five of us officers of the company were not much bothered by the wetness, we spent our evenings sitting on our duty cases in the tent behind a collection of wine bottles.

After a three day stay in the forest we moved back to Combles, where I moved into four small cellars with my platoon.

The first morning was relatively quiet, so I took a short walk through the devastated gardens and plundered trellises hung with delicious peaches. During my wanderings I came upon a house enclosed by high hedges, which must have been inhabited by a lover of beautiful antiques. On the walls of the rooms hung a collection of painted plates, as the Northern French love, holy water basins, copper engravings and wood-carved images of saints. Old china was stacked in large cupboards, beautiful leather-bound volumes, including a delicious old edition of Don Quixote, were scattered on the floor. It was a shame to see all of these treasures abandoned to ruin.

When I returned to my quarters, my men, who had also just returned from their own investigation of the gardens, had cooked a soup from canned meat, potatoes, peas, carrots, artichokes and many different kinds of leafy greens; it was such a thick soup that when you put the spoon in the handle would stay sticking straight up. While we were eating, a shell hit our house and three others nearby without even disturbing our meal. We were already too numb by the profusion of impressions. Bloody things must have already happened in the house; on a pile of rubble, in the central room, stood a crude cross with a series of names engraved on the wood. The next day, around noon, I went to the antique collector's house to fetch a volume of the illustrated supplements of the "Petit Journal," which are to be found in almost every French house; then I sat down in an untouched room, lit a small fire in the fireplace from pieces of furniture, and began to read. I could not help shaking my head often; I had put my hand, by accident, on the numbers printed at the time of the Faschoda affair. At about 7 o'clock, I had turned the last page and went into the anteroom in front of the entrance to the cellar, where my men were cooking on a small stove.

As soon as I arrived among them, there was a sharp bang at the front door, and at the same moment I felt a violent blow against my lower left leg. With the ancient cry of duelists, "Touched!" I jumped down the basement stairs, my shag pipe still in my mouth.

Lights were quickly turned on and the case was examined. We found a jagged hole gaped in my puttee, from which a stream of blood spurted to the ground. On the other side of my leg there was a roundish bulge of a shrapnel ball lodged under the skin. My men bandaged me up and carried me across the heavily shelled street to the catacombs, where our chief surgeon received me. While Lieutenant Wetje, who had rushed over, held my head, he cut out the shrapnel ball with knife and scissors, congratulating me, for the lead had passed sharply between my tibia and fibula without touching a bone. Habent sua fata libelli et balli (Books and bullets have their own destinies), the former medical student said with a grin as he left me with the nurse to be bandaged.

While lying on a stretcher in a niche of the catacombs until nightfall, many of my men came to check on me, to my delight. My revered Lieutenant Colonel von Oppen also came to visit me briefly.

That same evening I was carried with other wounded men to the end of the village where we were then loaded into an ambulance. Ignoring the screams of the occupants, the driver sped over craters and other obstacles on the road, which was under heavy fire, and finally handed us over to another ambulance that unloaded us in front of the church in the village of Fins, which was filled with hundreds of wounded. A nurse mentioned to me that in the last few weeks more than thirty thousand men had been treated there. From there I went to St. Quentin, whose windows were shaking from the incessant thunder of the battle, and then, in the hospital train, to Gera, where I found excellent care in the garrison hospital.

From comrades of the other battalions who were wounded after me, I learned the further fate of my company, which had moved back into position the day after I was wounded. After a loss-laden advance and a ten-hour barrage, it had been attacked from all sides as a result of the large gaps in the front. Little Schmidt, Ensign Wohlgemut, Lieutenants Vogel and Sievers, in short, almost all the comrades had met their deaths, fighting to the last second. Only a few survivors, among them Lieutenant Wetje, had fallen into the hands of the enemy; not a single one had returned to Combles to tell of the heroic struggle, which had been fought with such unbelievable bitterness. Even the English army's report made an honorable mention of the handful of German soldiers who had stood in fierce loyalty at Guillemont, to the last act.

Even though I was happy about the accidental hit that had miraculously saved me from certain death on the eve of the battle, I would have liked to share the fate of my comrades, as strange as it may sound to some, and let the iron die of war roll over me together with them. Always, at the climaxes of the bloody battles that I was to experience, the radiant, indelible glory of these fighters reminded me to prove myself worthy of the former comradeship.

*

* *

The days of Guillemont introduced me for the first time to the devastating effects of the material battle. We had to adapt to completely new forms of war. Every connection of the troops with the command, the artillery and the connecting regiments were paralyzed by the terrible fire. The signal runners fell victim to the hail of iron, the telephone wire, hardly pulled, was already chopped into pieces. Even the flashing signals of the signal lamps failed in the steamy, dust-clouded terrain. Behind the front line stretched a mile-wide zone where only the explosives ruled.

Even the regimental staff was unaware, until we returned after three days, where we had actually been and how the front was going. In these conditions, accurate artillery fire was impossible.

We were also completely unaware of the position of the English, although often, without knowing it, we were only a few meters apart. Sometimes a Tommy groping his way through the craters would run like an ant through a sandy path directly into a shell hole occupied by us, and vice versa, since our front line consisted of single, connectionless pieces that could easily be missed.

The landscape is unforgettable to those who have seen it. A short time ago, this area had consisted of villages, meadows, forests and fields, and now there was literally not a shrub, not a tiny stalk to be seen. Every hand's length of ground had been uprooted, again and again. The trees were uprooted, shredded and ground into mulch, the houses were blown away and pulverized into powder, the mountains were flattened and the farmland was turned into desert.

In this desert, surrounded by the dead and the thirsty, men struggled for days and weeks knowing that if they were wounded they would be hopelessly exposed to death by starvation.

The main blame for the immense losses in relation to the width of the attack front was borne by the rigid linear tactics carried out with old Prussian tenacity. Battalion after battalion was thrown into the crowded front line and rounded up in a few hours.

It was not until later that it was realized that things could not go on like this and stopped fighting for worthless strips of terrain in order to turn to a more mobile defense, the culmination of which became elastic zone tactics.

Therefore, never again was fighting fought with such dogged fervor as in those days, when people struggled for weeks over shattered patches of forest or unrecognizable ruins. The name of even the smallest Picardy nest recalls unheard-of heroic battles that are truly unique in world history. Only there the bloom of our disciplined youth sank into the dust. Sublime values, which had made the German people great, shone there once again in dazzling brilliance, only to slowly extinguish in a sea of mud and blood.

VIII

At St. Pierre~Vaast

AFTER spending fourteen days in the hospital and as many on leave, I rejoined the regiment, which was in position at Deuxnouds, very close to the well-known Grande Tranchée (Great Trench). We remained there for only two days after my arrival, and we spent two more days in the idyllic, ancient mountain village of Hattonchâtel. Then we steamed from the station of Mars-la-Tour again towards the region of the Somme.

We were unloaded in Bohain and put up in the nearby village of Brancourt. This area, which we would later visit many times, is predominantly inhabited by arable farmers, but there is a loom in almost every house. The population seemed to me unsympathetic, dirty, and on a low cultural and moral level. I was accommodated in a cottage occupied by a married couple and their daughter. I must admit that they prepared excellent egg dishes for me for my good money. The daughter told me right at the welcome coffee that she would have a good coffee with Poincaré after his return, that is, that she would give him a good talking to. Never have I heard anyone rant with such fluency as this filia hospitalis did in response to her neighbor's accusation of her having lived on a certain street in St. Quentin. "Ah, cette plure, cette pomme de terre pourrie, jetée sur un fumier, c'est la crème de la crème" (Ah, this rain, this rotten potato, thrown on a manure pile, it's the cream of the crop), she gushed, as she raced around the room with her hands outstretched like claws, unable to find an object to express her rage.

In the morning, when this Rose of Brancourt was busy preparing butter and doing other domestic chores, she looked incredibly uninviting, but in the afternoon, when it was time to strut up and down the village street or visit friends, the foul chrysalis had transformed into a magnificent butterfly. With a certain mistrust, I always looked at the large box full of rice powder, which was always on the table and seemed to completely replace water and soap.

Her father asked me one day to draw up an indictment for him to be sent to the local commander because a neighbor had grabbed him by the throat, beaten him, and threatened him with death, shouting, "Demande pardon!"

Such small observations gave me the comforting assurance that national pride is not a characteristic of the general public, even in France. This realization helped me two years later to get over the strange reception that some of our fellow countrymen gave us after four years of the hardest honorable fighting in our homeland. Il y a des cochons partout (There are pigs everywhere).

The 2nd Company was now led by Lieutenant Boje. We spent a number of days here that were embellished by good comradeship. I must confess that we often sat together in heavy drinking until we saw the whole world only as a ridiculous phantom circling around our table. There was also usually a tremendous noise coming from the boys' room. Those who have never been, in the short time span, between two murderous battles may judge it disparagingly, but in any case we wholeheartedly treated ourselves and our men to every hour of intoxication that we could wrest from life as long as it still held us within its circle.

For the coming operation I was designated as scout officer and was at the disposal of the division with a scouting party; two non-commissioned officers and four men.

On November 8th, in pouring rain, the battalion drove to the village of Gonnelieu, abandoned by the civilian population. From there the scouting party was detached to Liéramont and placed under the command of Rittmeister Böckelmann, head of division intelligence. The Rittmeister lived with us four scout officers, two observation officers and his adjutant in the spacious parsonage, in whose comfortably furnished rooms a comradely life together was led.

Our predecessors familiarized us with the division's position. We had to go to the front every other night. Our task was to define the position exactly, to check the connections and to orient ourselves with the environment in order to be able to brief troops in case of emergency and to carry out possible orders. The section assigned to me as a working area was located to the left of the St. Pierre-Vaast Forest, immediately in front of the so-called "Nameless Forest." On the first night, after almost drowning while wandering through a swamp crossed by the Tortille stream, I got caught in a dense cloud of phosgene gas, which sent me back to the Vaux forest with watery eyes, blinded by the fogged gas mask, falling into crater after crater.

On November 12th, hoping for better luck, I started my second walk forward with the order to determine the connections in the crater position. Along a chain of relay posts hidden in holes in the ground, I strove toward my goal.

The "crater position" bore its name rightly. On a plateau in front of the village of Rancourt, countless miniature craters were scattered, occupied here and there by a few men. The terrain made an impression of frightening desolation in its solitude, where only the whistling and crashing of bullets could be heard.

After some time I lost the connection to the crater line and went back in order to avoid running into the hands of the French. I came across a well-known officer from the 164th Regiment who warned me to not linger any longer in the dawning twilight. I therefore hastily crossed the "Nameless Forest" and stumbled through deep craters, over uprooted trees and an almost impenetrable tangle of downed branches.

When I stepped out of the edge of the forest, the sun had risen. The crater field laid before me without a trace of life. I stared, because in modern battle deserted areas are always suspicious.

Suddenly a shot fired by an invisible gunman hit both of my calves. I threw myself into the nearest crater and bandaged the wounds with my handkerchief, having of course forgotten my bandage pack again. A bullet had pierced my right calf and grazed my left.

With extreme caution, I crawled back into the woods and hobbled from there through the heavily shelled terrain to the dressing area.

Shortly before that, I experienced another example of how minor circumstances determine luck in war. About a hundred meters before a road junction, which I was heading for, the leader of a skirmishing division, with whom I had fought with in the 9th Company, called out to me. We had barely spoken for a minute when a grenade went off right in the middle of the intersection, which would probably have hit me if it hadn't been for this chance encounter.

After dark I was carried on a stretcher as far as Nurlu. Rittmeister Böckelmann was kindly waiting for me with a car. On the road, which was illuminated by enemy searchlights, the driver abruptly pulled the brake lever. A dark obstacle blocked the road. It was an infantry group with its commander, who had just fallen victim to a direct hit. The comrades lying united in death had the peaceful appearance of silent sleepers.

In the parish house I had to be carried into the cellar, because Liéramont was just getting his evening blessing. That same evening I was transported to the Villeret field hospital and from there to the Valenciennes military hospital.

The military hospital was set up in a Gymnasium building near the train station and housed over four hundred severely wounded. Day after day, funeral processions left through the main entrance to the muffled beat of drums. All the misery of the war seemed to be concentrated in this giant operating room. At a row of operating tables, the doctors carried out their bloody craft. Here a limb was amputated, there a skull was chiseled open, or a bandage was being loosened. Whimpers and cries of pain echoed through the room flooded by an implacable light, while white-robed nurses hurried busily from one table to the next with instruments or bandages.

Next to my bed laid a sergeant who had lost a leg and was dying. In his last hour he awoke from confused shivers and had his favorite chapter of the Bible read to him by the nurse. Then, in a barely audible voice, he apologized to all his parlor mates for having disturbed their rest so often with his fever deliriums and was dead in a few minutes, after having tried to imitate the comical dialect of our orderly in an effort to cheer us all up.

Half-healed after fourteen days, I was glad when I was finally able leave this place of collected misery. In the meantime, I had read with pride about the storm of the Fusilier Regiment against the St. Pierre-Vaast Forest, which had been so brilliantly executed.

The 111th Division still held the same position. As my train rolled into Epéhy, a series of explosions rang out. The twisted remains of freight cars scattered along the tracks made it clear how little there was to joke about.

"What's going on here?" asked a captain sitting opposite me, apparently freshly exported from home. Without stopping to answer him, I opened the compartment door and laid down behind the railroad embankment. Fortunately, these impacts were the last. Only a few horses were wounded.

Since I was not yet able to march well, I was assigned the post of observation officer. The observatory was on the sloping hillside between Nurlu and Moislains. It consisted of a scissor telescope built into a dugout, through which I could observe the front line, which I have come to know quite well. When the fire became stronger, when colored flares were raised or anything unusual happened, the division had to be notified by phone. For days I squatted freezing on a little chair behind the double eyepiece, immersed in the November fog, without any other diversion than a wire test now and then. If the wire ever broke, I had to have it mended by my malfunction squad.

The modern battlefield resembles an immense, dormant machinery, in which innumerable hidden eyes, ears and arms lie idly in wait for the one minute that matters most. Then, as a fiery overture, a single red flare rises from some hole in the earth, a thousand guns roar simultaneously. With a single catalyst the work of destruction, driven by countless levers, begins its crushing course.

Orders rose, as sparks and lightning through a tightly-meshed net, to spur on increased destruction in front, to set new men and new material in motion from behind in a steady stream, and to hurl them into the surf. Everyone feels as if they're gripped by a whirlpool from far away, by a mysterious will, and driven with relentless precision to the focal points of deadly events.

Every twenty-four hours another officer would come to relieve me; I would then return to rest in the nearby village of Nurlu, where relatively comfortable quarters were established in a vast, deep wine cellar. I still sometimes remember the long, pensive November evenings I spent, smoking my pipe, lonely in front of the fireplace of the small, barrel-shaped cellar vault, while outside in the desolate park the mist dripped from bare trees and at long pauses an echoing thud interrupted the silence.

On December 18th, the division was relieved and I rejoined the regiment, which laid at rest in the village of Fresnoy-le-Grand. There I took over the command of the 2nd Company for Lieutenant Boje, who was on leave. In Fresnoy the regiment had four weeks of undisturbed rest, and everyone strove to profit from it as much as possible. Christmas and New Year were celebrated by large company parties at which beer and grog flowed in torrents. There were just five men left in the 2nd Company who had celebrated the previous Christmas with me in the trenches of Monchy.

I lived with Ensign Gornick and my brother Fritz, who had joined the regiment for six weeks as an ensign, in the so-called salon and two bedrooms of a small French pensioner. We made fun of the stuffy couple, who guarded their plush furniture and marrow bouquets as well as the wood stock piled up in the courtyard with real suspicious eyes and lived on a constant war footing with the boys.

The cup was brandished more than ever in the little nest. Walking through the narrow streets late at night, one could hear the turmoil of merry revelry everywhere from the quarters of enlisted men, non-commissioned officers and officers. In war, everything is calculated for reckless effect, which is probably where the field soldier's predilection for alcohol in its concentrated forms came from. Intercourse with the civilian population was sometimes of undesirable confidentiality; Venus deprived Mars of many a servant.

Of course, service was immediately resumed in old Prussian strictness, and it was an excellent sign for leader and troop that after fourteen days manliness was back to the old level.

During the first week there was a review by the division commander, Major General Sontag, at which the regiment was praised for its outstanding conduct in the storming of the St. Pierre-Vaast Forest and received numerous commendations. When I presented the 2nd Company to the division commander at parade march, I noticed that Lieutenant Colonel von Oppen appeared to report on me to the general. A few hours later I was ordered to division staff headquarters, where the general presented me with the 1st Class Iron Cross.

On January 17, 1917, I left Fresnoy to attend a four-week training course for company commanders at the French military training camp in Sissonne, near Laon. The leader of the detachment to which I was attached, Captain Funk, made sure that the service was, in the end, thoroughly enjoyable. He had a special ability to reduce the countless regulations to a few extremely simple rules.

The rations during this time were probably the most scarce I experienced during the war. During the entire four weeks, there was rarely anything on the tables of our huge mess hall other than thin turnip greens. And the service was by no means easy.

IX

The Somme Retreat

RETURING to the regiment, which had been in position for several days at the ruins of Villers-Carbonnel, I was given the command of the 8th Company as a substitute. Resting place was the motto.

When marching from there to the front, one had to cross the lowlands of the Somme at the villages of Brie and St. Christ, whose bleak desolation amidst the melancholy swampland put me in a sad mood, especially at night, when dark wisps of clouds chased across the moonlit sky, adding to the impression of chaos by eerie differences in brightness.

The position was subjected to numerous English advances during the last period of our stay, which were connected with our eagerly prepared great clearing of the Somme area. The enemy sent a combat patrol against our line almost every morning to make sure of our presence. I bring here some experiences of that period:

On March, 4, 1917, in the afternoon, there was a lively fire fight due to the clear weather. One heavy battery in particular, under balloon observation, almost completely leveled the section of my third platoon. In order to complete my position map, I patched through the completely sodden "nameless trench" to the third platoon in the afternoon. During this walk I saw the huge yellow sun sink into the earth in front of us, trailing a long black plume of smoke. A dashing aviator had approached the unpleasant tethered balloon and shot it on fire. He managed to escape despite furious pursuit fire.

In the evening, Fusilier Schnau came to me and reported that he had heard a pecking noise under his group dugout for four days. I passed on this observation and was given an engineer detachment with listening devices, which, however, did not perceive anything suspicious. Later we learned that at that time the whole position was supposed to have been undermined.

On March 5th, in the early morning hours, an enemy patrol approached our trench and began to cut through the wire entanglement. Alerted by a sentry, Lieutenant Eisen rushed with some men, threw some hand grenades which forced the enemy to retreat, leaving two of their men on the ground. One of them, a young lieutenant, died shortly thereafter; the other, a sergeant, was seriously wounded in the arm and leg. From the officer's papers we learned that his name was Stokes and he belonged to the 2nd Royal Munster Fusilier Regiment of the British Army. He was very well dressed, and his face, cramped from death, was intelligently and vigorously cut. We buried him behind our trench and placed a simple cross for him. That incident served to make me realize that not all patrol actions can end as happily as mine had.

The next morning, after a brief artillery preparation, the English attacked the section of the neighboring company in which Lieutenant Reinhardt commanded, with fifty men. The enemy had crept in front of the wire, and after giving a signal with a white piece of cloth that one of them wore on his sleeve to silence their machine guns, they launched themselves, with the last shots of the artillery, against our trench. All of them had blackened their faces with soot in order to stand out as little as possible in the darkness.

Our men, however, received them so masterfully that only one got into the trench. This one immediately ran through to the second line, where he was shot down after not heeding the order to surrender. Only one lieutenant and one sergeant managed to jump the wire. The lieutenant fell even though he was wearing body armor under his uniform, because a pistol shot by Reinhardt at point-blank range had driven a piece of metal from the body armor into his belly. The sergeant's legs were almost torn off completely by the hand grenades, but he managed to hold his short pipe clenched between his teeth until his stoic death.

On the morning of that successful day, I strolled through my trench and saw Lieutenant Pfaffendorf on a sentry post, directing the fire of his mortars from there with a scissor binoculars. I stepped next to him and immediately noticed an Englishman crossing cover behind the third enemy line, standing out sharply against the horizon in his khaki brown uniform. I snatched the rifle from the nearest sentry's hand, set sights at six hundred yards, took sharp aim at the man's head and pulled the trigger. He took three more steps, then fell on his back as if his legs had been pulled out from under him, flapped his arms a few times, and rolled into a shell crater from which we could see his brown sleeve gleaming through the lens for a long time.

On March 9th, our section was heavily shelled. I had one dead and several wounded. The entrance to my shelter was crushed like a matchbox. In the evening we were relieved and began our march.

On the 13th, I received the honorable order from Colonel von Oppen to hold the company section with a patrol of two groups until the regiment had completely crossed the Somme. Each of the four sections in the front line was to be manned by such a patrol, the command of which was entrusted to energetic officers. The sections were under the command of Lieutenants Reinhardt, Fischer, Lorek and myself from the right wing. The village homes we passed on our march forward had taken on the appearance of madhouses. Whole companies were knocking down walls or sitting on top of the roofs and smashing the tiles. Trees were cut down, windows were smashed, clouds of dust and smoke rose from enormous piles of rubble all around, in short, an orgy of destruction was being celebrated.

You could see men wearing suits and women's dresses that were left behind by the inhabitants, top hats on their heads, racing around full of incredible zeal. With the ingenuity of the destroyer, they would locate the main supporting beams of the houses, attach ropes to it and, with the tactful shouting and great effort, pulled until everything came crashing down. Others wielded huge hammers and smashed everything in their path, from the flowerpot in front of the window sill to the elaborate glass construction of a conservatory.

By the time the Siegfried position was reached, every village was a heap of rubble, every tree felled, every road undermined, every well polluted, every river course dammed, every cellar blown up or booby trapped with hidden bombs, all supplies and metals were carried back, every rail dismantled, every telephone wire unwound, everything combustible burned; in short, the region awaiting the advancing enemy had been transformed into a barren desert.

The moral justification of these destructions is much disputed, but the chauvinistic howls of rage seem to me more understandable this time than the satisfied applause of the home warriors and newspaper writers. Where thousands of peaceful people are deprived of their homes, the smug sense of power must remain silent.

As a Prussian officer, I am naturally not in doubt for a moment about the necessity of the deed. Waging war means trying to destroy the enemy through the ruthless use of force. War is the hardest of crafts, its masters may only open their hearts to humanity as long as it cannot harm them.

That this action, which the hour demanded, was not beautiful, does not matter. The attentive observer could already see it from the way in which the objective will of the leader translated into a series of lower instincts in the crew.

The 2nd Company left the position on the 13th, which I took over with my two groups. That night a man with the ominous name Kirchhof was killed by a shot to the head. Oddly enough, this unlucky bullet was the only one shot by the enemy within several hours.

I ordered everything possible to deceive the enemy about our actual strength. A few shovelfuls of earth were thrown over the slope of the trench, some here and some there, and our one machine gun fired a number of rounds from the right and then from the left. Nevertheless, our fire sounded quite thin when low-flying planes crossed the position or when a detachment of entrenchers crossed the enemy rear. Consequently, patrols appeared every night at various points in front of our trench to tamper with the wire.

The day before last I almost met an annoying end. The dud of an anti-balloon gun whizzed down from a tremendous height and exploded on the parapet against which I had been leaning unsuspectingly. I was hurled by the air pressure right into the opposite entrance of a tunnel, where I found myself extremely perplexed.

On the 17th, in the morning, we realized that an attack must be imminent. In the heavily muddy English front line trench, otherwise unoccupied, the sound of many soggy boots was heard. The laughing and shouting of a strong detachment revealed that they must have also moistened themselves inside as well. Dark figures approached our wire and were driven away by gunfire, one collapsed wailing and remained lying. I drew my men together in a huddle around the mouth of a running trench and endeavored to illuminate the foreland with flares while the enemy's artillery fire began to rain down on us. Since we soon ran out of white flares, we launched a veritable fireworks display of different colored flares. At 5 o'clock, the hour of the ordered evacuation dawned, we quickly blew up our shelters with hand grenades, as far as they had not yet been equipped with the ingeniously constructed infernal machines.

At the appointed time, all patrols, even those already engaged in hand grenade fights, retreated towards the Somme. As soon as the last of us crossed the lowlands, the bridges were blown up by engineer commandos. The drum fire was still raging on our position. Only after several hours did the first enemy patrols appear on the Somme. We retreated behind the Siegfried position, which was still under construction; the battalion took up quarters in the village of Lehaucourt, situated on the "Canal de St. Quentin." I lived with my orderly in a small, cozy cottage, where the household goods of the exiled inhabitants were still stored in chests and cupboards. As a characteristic trait for the nature of our people I would like to mention that my lad, the faithful Knigge, could not be persuaded, despite all coaxing, to set up his night's camp in the warm living room, but instead he wanted to sleep in the cold kitchen. This restraint, typical of the Lower Saxon, made intercourse with the crew much easier for the leader. Discipline in the regiment only loosened when we had to hire members of other tribes as replacements.

On the first evening of rest, I invited my friends to a mulled wine flavored with all the spices left by the owner of the house, because our retreat to the Somme had resulted not only in the praise of all our superiors, but also in a fortnight's vacation.

X

In the Village of Fresnoy

MY leave, which I started a few days later, was not interrupted this time. On April 9, 1917, I rejoined the 2nd Company, which was quartered in the village of Merignies, not far from Douai. The joy of reunion was disturbed by an unexpected alarm, which made me particularly uncomfortable when the order was given to lead the battle train to Beaumont. Through rain showers and snow flurries I rode at the head of the column of wagons creeping across the Chaussée (roadway) until finally reaching our destination at 1 o'clock in the morning.

After I had accommodated horses and men in the most makeshift way, I went in search of quarters for myself, but I found that even the smallest place had already been occupied. Finally, a field superintendent had the bright idea of offering me his bed, since he had to keep watch on the telephone. While I threw myself on it with boots and spurs, he told me that the English had taken the Vimy Heights and a large piece of terrain from the Bavarians. Despite his hospitality, I could tell that he was extremely unhappy about the transformation of his quiet little village into a rendezvous place for combat troops.

The following morning the battalion marched towards the cannon thunder as far as the village of Fresnoy. There I was ordered to set up an observation post. Together with some men I chose a small house on the western edge of the village, through the roof of which I had a lookout built facing the front. We moved our living quarters into the cellar, and when we cleared it out, a sack of potatoes fell into our hands as a pleasant addition to our extremely meager rations. Lieutenant Gornick, who had already evacuated the village of

Villerwal and was holding a platoon as a field guard, also sent me a large can of liverwurst and several bottles of red wine as a comradely gift from the supplies he had hastily left behind. I sent an expedition group armed with baby carriages and similar means of transport to recover all of these treasures which, unfortunately, had to turn back without having achieved anything, since the English had already reached the edge of the village with dense lines of infantry units.

On April 14th, I received the order to set up a news collection point in the village. For this purpose I was provided with messengers, cyclists, telephones, telegraphs, carrier pigeons and a chain of signal lights. That same evening I looked for a suitable cellar with a built-in tunnel and then went for the last time to my old quarters located on the western edge of the village.

During the night I thought I heard a few crashes and screams from my lad, but I was so drowsy that I only muttered, "Let them shoot!" and rolled over to the other side, even though the whole room was thick with dust. The next morning I was awakened by Colonel von Oppen's nephew, little Schultz, shouting, "Man, don't you know that the whole house has collapsed?" When I got up and looked at the damage, I noticed that a heavy shell had burst at the top of the roof, destroying all of the rooms, including my observatory post. If the fuse had been a little coarser, the projectile would have stuck to the walls of our cellar. Schultz told me that his orderly, on seeing the destroyed house, had said: "There was a lieutenant living in there yesterday, let's go see if there is anything left of him." My lad was beside himself over my incredibly deep sleep.

In the morning we moved to our new cellar. On the way there, we were almost hit by the debris of a collapsing church tower, which had been blown up by a sapper commando so that the enemy artillery couldn't use it as a reference point. In a neighboring village, they had even forgotten to notify the two sentries who were watching from the tower hatch. Miraculously, the men were pulled out of the ruble unharmed.

We settled into our spacious cellar quite comfortably, dragging together pieces of furniture from the castle and cottage that seemed practical at the time.

Throughout the days a series of fierce aerial battles took place overhead, almost always ending in the defeat of the English, as the Richthofen fighter squadron circled over the area. Often five or six planes in succession were either forced to land or shot down in flames. Once we saw an occupant fly out in a wide arc and crash to the earth as a black dot separated from his plane. Staring up, however, also had its dangers; for example, a man of the 4th Company was fatally hit in the neck by a falling piece of shrapnel.

On April 18th, I visited the 2nd Company in position, which laid in an arc around the village of Arleux. Lieutenant Boje told me that so far he had had only one wounded man, since the predictable firing pattern of the English allowed us to calculate when the best time was to evacuate the areas that were about to be shelled.

After wishing him well, I had to leave the village at a gallop because of the heavy shells that continuously fell. Three hundred meters behind Arleux, I stopped and looked at the clouds of high splashing impacts, which, depending on whether brick walls were crushed or garden soil was thrown up, were colored red and black, mixed with the subtle white of the bursting shrapnel. However, when several volleys of small caliber shells fell on the narrow trails that connected Arleux to Fresnoy, I abandoned the quest for impressions and hastily cleared the field, so as not to be "shot," as was the common technical term of the 2nd Company.

I embarked on such walks, some of which I extended to the little town of Henin-Liétard, quite often, since in the first fourteen days, despite my large number of personnel, there was not a single dispatch to carry out.

Beginning on April 20th, Fresnoy was shelled by an extremely large caliber cannon, whose shells howled down with an almost infernal roar. After each impact, the village was enveloped in a huge, reddish-brown cloud of picric acid. A man of the 9th Company located in the castle courtyard, surprised by such a projectile, was hurled high above the trees in the park and broke almost every bone when he hit the ground.

In the afternoons the village was under a fire of various calibers. Despite the danger, I could not tear myself away from the skylight of my quarters, for it was a thrilling sight to see individual detachments and signalmen hurrying, often throwing themselves, across the shelled terrain, while to right and left of them the ground is spurting up.

From day to day, the artillery activity became livelier and ruled out any doubt of an attack in the near future. At midnight on the 27th, I received the message: "Sixty-seven from five a.m.," which, according to our numerical code, meant "increased alert from five a.m."

So, in order to be equal to the anticipated exertions, I immediately laid down, but just as I was about to fall asleep, a shell hit the house, crushed the wall of the cellar stairs, and threw all the masonry into the room for us. We jumped up and rushed into the tunnel.

As we squatted on the stairs, weary and tired, by the light of a candle, the leader of my signalmen, whose station and two valuable signal lamps had been smashed in the afternoon, came running up and reported: "Lieutenant, the cellar of house No. 11 has taken a direct hit, there are still some lying under the rubble!" Since I had two cyclists and three telephonists lying in that house, I rushed with some men to help.

I found a corporal and a wounded man there in the tunnel and received the following report: When the first shots struck suspiciously close, four of the five inhabitants decided to go into the tunnel. One jumped down immediately, one remained sleeping quietly on his bed, while the others decided to first put on their boots. The most cautious and the most indifferent got off well, as so often in war, the first one that jumped down the tunnel was completely without wound, the sleeping one had a piece of shrapnel in his thigh. The other three were torn apart when the shell smashed through the cellar wall, exploding in the opposite corner.

I lit a cigar just in case and stepped into the smoke-filled cellar, in the middle of which a desolate pile of debris of broken beds, straw sacks, and other pieces of furniture arched up almost to the ceiling. After tucking a few lights between the wall joints, we set about our sad task. We grabbed the limbs sticking out of the rubble and pulled the bodies out. The head of one man had been cut off and the neck sat atop the torso like a big bloody sponge. From the stump of a second man's arm was a protruding bone, and the uniform was soaked with the blood from a large chest wound. The third had his guts spilling out of his torn abdomen. As we pulled him out, a splintered piece of board that was lodged in the gruesome wound produced a nasty sound. One of the orderlies made a remark about it and was ordered to be quiet by my lad, Knigge: "Keep quiet! There's no use yapping about such things!"

I took an inventory of the valuables found on the bodies. It was an eerie business. The candles flickered reddish through the thick haze while the two men handed me wallets and silver objects as if in some secret, dark ritual. The fine yellow brick dust had settled on the faces of the dead, giving them the rigid appearance of wax masks. We threw blankets over them and hurried out of the cellar, having laid our wounded man onto a tent canvas. With the stoic advice, "Grit your teeth, comrade!" we dragged him through a wild fire fight to the medical shelter.

Returning to my quarters, I first fortified myself with a number of sherry brandies, for the events had nevertheless got on my nerves. Soon we got another lively fire and quickly gathered in the shelter, since we had just seen the effects of the artillery in the cellars and still had the horrifying image of it in our minds.

At 5:14 a.m., the fire swelled to unbelievable strength in just a few seconds. Our shelter swayed and shook like a ship on a stormy sea; the bursting of masonry and the crashing of neighboring houses resounded from every direction.

At 7 o'clock I caught a light message from the brigade to the 2nd Battalion: "Brigade wants immediate clarification of the situation." After an hour a dispatch runner brought me back the message: "Enemy occupied Arleux and Arleux Park. Set 8th Company to counterattack, no word so far. — Captain Rocholl."

This was the only, albeit very important, message I had passed on with my huge apparatus of liaison during the three weeks of my stay in Fresnoy. Now, when my activity was of greatest value, the artillery had put almost all of my equipment out of operation. These were the consequences of over-centralization.

This surprising reconnaissance made me understand why infantry rounds being fired from a fairly close range had been clattering against the walls for some time now.

We were hardly aware of the regiment's great losses when the shelling began with renewed force. My lad was the last one standing on the top shelter step when a thunderclap announced that the English had finally succeeded in shooting into our cellar. The good lad Knigge was hit with a rough stone in his back, but otherwise took no damage. Upstairs, everything had been smashed to bits. Daylight reached us through two bicycles pressed into the tunnel entrance. We retreated rather meekly to the lowest step, while dull vibrations and the continually rumbling of stones convinced us of the insecurity of our cellar.

Miraculously, the telephone was still undamaged; I presented our inexpedient situation to the chief of divisional communications and was ordered to retreat with the men to the nearby medical shelter.

So we packed up our most necessary things and prepared to leave the cellar through the second still preserved exit. In spite of my energetic orders, supported by unambiguous threats, the less warlike men of the telephone company were still hesitant to leave the cover of the shelter, until that entrance, also hit by a large caliber shell, buckled with a great crash. Fortunately, no one was hit, only our little dog howled miserably and disappeared from that moment on.

We tore aside the bicycles blocking the exit to the cellar, crawled on all fours over the pile of rubble and gained the open air through a narrow gap in the wall. Without stopping to contemplate the incredible transformation of the place within these few hours, we ran towards the exit of the village. The last one had hardly left the courtyard gate when the house was hit again by a powerful impact.

The terrain between the edge of the village and the medical shelter was being pounded with a barrage of fire. Light and heavy shells, short and delayed fuses, duds, cartridges and shrapnel combined to create a frenzy of acoustic and visual effects. In between, dodging the village's infernal cauldron to the left and right, support troops pushed forward.

In Fresnoy, one spurting column of earth replaced another, each one seeming trying to trump the previous one. As if by magic, one house after another was sucked into the ground; walls broke, roofs collapsed, and bare rafter frames were hurled through the air, mowing down the neighboring roofs. Clouds of splinters danced above whitish vapor. Our eyes and ears were transfixed by this swirling chaos of destruction.

In the medical tunnel we spent two more days in agonizing confinement, because apart from my men it was also populated by two battalion commands, relief detachments and the inevitable "stragglers." The heavy traffic in front of the entrances did not go unnoticed, of course. Soon sharply aimed shells began to fall at one-minute intervals, wounding a few men every time. I lost four bicycles, which we had placed next to the entrance to the tunnel, to this unpleasant shooting. They were bent into strange shapes and thrown to the wind.

In front of the entrance, stiffly and silently wrapped in a canvas, his big horn-rimmed glasses still on his face, laid the leader of the 8th Company, Lieutenant Lemière, whom his men had brought here. He had been shot in the mouth. Strangely, his younger brother died a few months later from the exact same injury.

On April 30th, my successor from the relieving 25th Regiment took over and we moved off to Flers, the staging area of the 1st Battalion. Leaving the lime quarry "Chez-bon-temps" with its heavy impacts on the left, we strolled soulfully through the beautiful afternoon along the dirt road to Beaumont. The eyes again enjoyed the beauty of the earth and the lungs became intoxicated with the mild spring air, glad to have escaped the unbearable confinement of the cellar. With the thunder of the cannons behind me, I felt the poet's words:

> Truly a day made by God,
> To better things than to fight.

In Flers, I found the quarters assigned to me occupied by some sergeants of the rear, who refused to make room under the pretext of having to guard the room for a Baron von X., but did not reckon with the extremely tense nerves of a tired front-line soldier. I had my companions break down the door without further ado, and after a small scuffle, in front of the frightened inhabitants of the house, who had rushed over in their night clothes, the gentlemen were thrown down the stairs. My lad Knigge's politeness even went so far as to hurl their high boots at them. After this little brawl, I climbed into the warmed bed, half of which I offered to my friend Kius, who was wandering around without quarters. The sleep in this long-desired furniture did us so much good that we awoke the next morning "in old freshness."

Since the 1st Battalion had suffered the fewest casualties during the last few days of fighting, the mood was excellent as we marched to the Douai station. From there we drove to the railroad junction Busigny, which was near the village of Sérain, where we were to rest for a few days. There we found decent quarters with the friendly population, and already on the first evening the cheerful noise of comradely reunions came from many houses.

This libation after a happily passed battle is one of the most beautiful memories of veteran warriors.

And if ten of the dozen had fallen, the two survivors would gather over a bottle on the first night of rest, empty a glass in silence at the memory of their departed comrades and jokingly discuss their shared experiences. The survived dangers of the lansquenet, the future sip from a full bottle, whether death and the devil grinned at it, so long as the wine was good. This has always been the right custom of war.

That made the officer's table especially worthwhile to me. Here, where the spiritual bearers and pioneers of the front came together, the will to victory was concentrated and became form in the features of weather-hardened faces. Here was alive an element which underlined and yet spiritualized the desolateness of war, which was so seldom found among the people with whom one laid in the craters, the sporting joy of danger, the chivalrous urge to prevail in a fight. At least I never heard a word of hesitation in this much maligned circle.

The next morning my lad Knigge appeared and read me the orders, from which it became clear to me around noon that I was to take over the command of the 4th Company. In this company, the poet Hermann Löns from Lower Saxony had fallen in the fall of 1914.

XI

Against the Indians

ON May 6, 1917, we were already on the march again to the well-known Brancourt, and the following day we moved through Montbréhain, Ramicourt, Joncourt to the Siegfried position, which we had left only a month ago.

The first evening was stormy; heavy rain showers beat down incessantly on the flooded terrain. Soon, however, a series of beautiful, warm days reconciled us to our new abode.

Our position formed a crescent-shaped salient in front of the St. Quentin canal, behind which laid the famous Siegfried position. It was puzzling to me why we had to lie down in the narrow, imperfect clay trenches while we had the giant, mighty bulwark behind us.

The front line meandered through an idyllic meadow landscape shaded by small clumps of trees in the soft colors of spring. One could move with impunity behind and in front of the trenches, as numerous field guards miles ahead have secured the position. These postings were a thorn in the side of the enemy, and not a night went by in many a week when they did not attempt to drive out the small crews here or there by trickery or force.

However, our first period of position passed in pleasant peace; the weather was so fine that the men spent the warm nights lying outside in the grass. On May 14th, we were relieved by the 8th Company and, with the burning St. Quentin on our right, moved to our resting place in Montbréhain, a large village that had suffered little from the war and consequently had very comfortable quarters. On the 20th we occupied the Siegfried position as a reserve company. We had the purest summer holiday, during the day we sat in the numerous arbors built into the embankment or bathed and rowed in the canal.

The disadvantage of such ideal positions is the frequent visit of superiors, which is not appreciated by the men, especially in the trenches. However, my left wing, bordering the village of Bellenglise, was by no means complaining about a lack of enemy fire. On the very first day, one of my men was hit in the right buttock by a piece of shrapnel. When I rushed to the scene of the accident, he was already sitting on his left side, drinking a cup of coffee and eating a huge jam sandwich, waiting for the medics.

On May 25th, we relieved the 12th Company at the Riqueval Farm. This farm, a former large estate, served as a base for one of the four companies that occupied the position. Three machine gun nests scattered in the rear terrain were to be occupied by one group each. These fighting nests, grouped like a checkerboard behind the fighting position, were the first attempts at elastic defense.

The rest of the people were sent forward at night for entrenchment duties.

The farm was at most one thousand five hundred meters behind the front line, yet its buildings, enclosed by an overgrown park, were still completely untouched. It was also densely inhabited, since the tunnels were still under construction. The paths in the park surrounded by flowering hedges and the beauty of the environment gave our existence, despite the proximity of the front, a trace of that serene enjoyment of life which the Frenchman understands by his "vie de campagne." A pair of swallows had taken up residence in my bedroom and began noisily feeding their insatiable offspring in the early hours of the morning.

On May 30th, this idyll came to an end for me, because Lieutenant Vogeley, who had been discharged from the military hospital, again took over the command of the 4th Company. I joined my old 2nd Company in the trenches, which was currently under the command of a cavalry lieutenant.

Our section was occupied by two platoons from the Roman road to the so-called Artillery Trench; the company commander was situated with the 3rd Company behind a small slope about two hundred meters back. There was also a tiny wooden hut, which I occupied together with Lieutenant Kius, trusting in the dispersion of the English artillerymen. One side was glued to a small hillside, parallel to the direction of fire, the other three were defiantly flanking the enemy. Every day, when the morning greeting came, one could hear the following conversation between the occupants of the upper and lower bunk:

"Hey, Ernst!"

"Huh?"

"I think they're shooting!"

"Well, let's lay here a little longer; I think those were the last shots."

After fifteen minutes:

"Hey, Oskar!"

"Yes?"

"It hasn't stopped at all today; I think a shrapnel bullet just went through the wall. We'd better get up. The artillery observer next door left a while ago!"

We had always carelessly taken off our boots. When we were ready, the Englishman usually was as well, and we could sit down merrily at the ridiculously small table, drink the coffee that had turned sour from the heat, and light the morning cigar. In the afternoon, we would mockingly sunbath in the tented area in front of the door of the English artillery.

Our pad was also extremely entertaining in other respects. When lying on the wire cot in dolce far niente, huge earthworms shuttled along the earthen wall, shooting into their holes with incredible speed when disturbed. A grizzled mole sniffed out of his burrow from time to time and did much to enliven our extended siesta.

On June 12th, I had to occupy the field guard, attached to our company's section, with twenty men. At a late hour we left the position and walked into the warm evening on a trail that snaked through the undulating terrain. Dusk had advanced so far that the red poppies in the overgrown fields blended into the bright green grass in a strangely rich hue. We strolled silently across the flowery ground, each occupied with his own thoughts, with our rifles slung, and after twenty minutes had reached our destination. Whispering, the guard was handed over, the posts were quietly set up, and then the relieved crew disappeared into the darkness.

The field guard leaned against a small steep slope. In the back, a tangled patch of forest flowed into the night, separated from the slope by a hundred-meter-wide strip of meadow. In front of it and on the right flank rose two hills on which the English line ran. Between these hills a trench led to the enemy.

There, while dropping off my sentries, I met Vice-Sergeant Hackmann with some people from the 7th Company about to go on a patrol. I joined them as a battle buddy, although I was not actually allowed to leave my post.

Using a method of action I had invented, we crossed two wire entanglements blocking the way and, strangely enough, without encountering a sentry, made it over the crest of the hill where we could hear Englishmen entrenching to our left and right. Later it became clear to me that the enemy had withdrawn his postings in order to not affect them during the fire attack on our outpost, which I will report on in a moment.

The way of approach to which I have just alluded consisted in making each member of the patrol advance, alternately, crawling on his belly over the terrain along which he could, at any moment, meet the enemy. Thus, at any given time, only one whom fate might choose was in danger of being shot by a lurking gunman, while the others were united further back ready to intervene. Of course, I never used to exclude myself from this service, although I considered my presence at the patrol more important. However, in wartime, the front-line officer must sometimes make tactical mistakes for subjective reasons.

We skirted several entrenching divisions, which were unfortunately separated from us by dense obstacles. After the sergeant's somewhat eccentric suggestion to try and pass himself off as a defector and negotiate until he had bypassed the first enemy post was rejected in a short consultation, we stalked sullenly back to the field guard.

When we reached the outpost I sat down on my coat on the steep slope, lit my pipe as carefully as I could and let my imagination run wild. In the midst of the most beautiful castle in the area, I was startled by a peculiar rustling sound coming from the copse. The senses are always on the lookout for enemies, and it is strange that at such moments, when there are no unusual sounds at all, one immediately knows for certain: something is going on!

Immediately the sentry from the neighboring outpost came rushing up, "Lieutenant, there are seventy Englishmen advancing towards the edge of the woods!"

I wondered a bit about the precise numbers given, but took the precaution of hiding on the top of the steep slope in the high grass with four other men, in order to observe the further development of things. After a few seconds I saw a troop scurrying across the meadow. While my men were pointing their rifles at him, I called out a soft, "Who goes there?" It was the sergeant Teilengerdes, a veteran warrior of the 2nd Company, who was trying to gather his excited group.

I quickly gathered everyone together and formed a firing line, with the right wing resting against the steep slope and left against the edge of the copse. In an instant, the men were ready with their bayonets mounted. When I checked the position and tried to reprimand a man standing a bit behind us, I got the answer: "I am a stretcher-bearer." The man had his drill regulations well in mind. Reassured by this triumph of Prussian discipline, I had him fall in.

While we were crossing the strip of meadow, a hail of shrapnel and wild machine-gun crackling started from the English side. We automatically switched to a running pace to gain the blind spot of the hill ahead.

Suddenly, a dark shadow rose in front of me. I tore off a hand grenade and hurled it at him. To my horror, through the flash of the explosion, I recognized Teilengerdes, the sergeant, who had run forward and tripped over a wire, unnoticed. Fortunately he was unharmed. At the same time the sharper crack of English hand grenades resounded next to us, and the shrapnel fire intensified to an unpleasant density.

My firing line fluttered and disappeared in the direction of the escarpment, which was under heavy fire, while I kept my place with Teilengerdes and three faithfuls. Suddenly someone nudged me, "The English!"

As if in a dream, for a few seconds, the meadow was illuminated only by darting sparks, two strings of kneeling figures bored into my eyes, rose and then advanced. I clearly recognized the figure of the officer on the right wing.

We jumped up and ran towards the steep slope. Although I stumbled over a treacherous wire stretched through the high grass, I arrived at my destination without further incident and brought my excited men into a firing line. We pressed ourselves together as close as possible, rifle to rifle, and took aim at the copse.

I have always experienced that at such moments the ordinary man, who is fully occupied with his personal danger, admires the apparently uninvolved objectivity of the leader who, amidst the thousand unnerving impressions of battle, has the execution of his mission clearly in mind. This admiration lifts every chivalrous man above himself and spurs him on to ever greater achievements, so that leader and crew ignite each other to a tremendous display of energy. The moral factor is everything.

The fire died down abruptly, while multiple crackling and rustling sounds slipped through the undergrowth of the copse.

"Stop! Who goes there?! Password?!"

We yelled for five minutes and also shouted the old slogan of the 1st Battalion, "Lüttje Lage," an expression for schnapps and beer, familiar to every Hanoverian; but we were answered only by a strange, incomprehensible shouting. At last I took the responsibility upon myself and ordered the men to fire, although some men claimed to have heard German words. Bullets from twenty rifles swept into the copse, the chambers rattled, and soon the shouting over there had turned into whimpering. I had a sinking feeling of uncertainty.

But yellow flames flashed at us from time to time. One of us got shot in the shoulder and was immediately bandaged by the medic.

"Cease Fire!"

Slowly the command filtered through and the fire stopped. The tension of the nerves was dampened by the act.

Renewed shouting of the password and on my part the persuasive request: "Come here, you are prisoners, hands up!"

Over there, many voices shouted. One of them detached himself from the edge of the forest and came towards us. One of us made the foolish mistake of shouting "Password!" at him, whereupon he stopped and turned around.

"Shoot him!"

A dozen shots; the figure slumped and slid into the tall grass.

This little interlude filled us with a feeling of satisfaction. From the edge of the forest, confused shouting resounded again; it sounded as if the attackers were encouraging each other to take action against the mysterious defenders.

We stared at the dark strip in the greatest suspense. It began to dawn, and a light mist rose from the bottom of the meadow.

Then a row of shadows rose out of the darkness. Five, ten, fifteen, a whole chain. With trembling hands we released the safety from our rifles. They were within fifty meters, thirty, fifteen . . . . Fire! For minutes the guns rattled. Sparks flew up when splattering lead slugs smashed against weapons and steel helmets.

Suddenly a shout: "Aaaattention, left!" A crowd of attackers sped toward us from the far left, preceded by a giant figure with a revolver outstretched, wielding a white club.

"Left group, pivot left!"

The men quickly turned around and, while standing, received the attackers. Some of the opponents, including the leader, collapsed under the hastily fired shots, the others disappeared without a trace, as quickly as they had come.

This was the moment to go for the kill. With our side arms raised and furious hurrahs, we stormed the copse. Hand grenades flew into the tangled undergrowth, and in no time we were back in possession of our field guard, though, without having grabbed the sleek enemy.

We gathered in an adjacent cornfield and stared into each other's pale, sleepy faces. The sun had risen, brilliantly. A lark soared high and annoyed us with its trilling. We were in about the same mood in which one throws the cards on the table after a full night of gambling, when the cool morning air through the open windows mingles with stale cigar smoke.

While we offered each other our canteens and lit our cigarettes, we heard the enemy moving away through the hollow way, along with their loudly moaning wounded.

I decided to walk down the battlefield. Strange shouts and cries of pain rose from the grass area where our firing line had shot up. We discovered a row of dead men in the tall grass and three wounded men begging us for mercy. They seemed firmly convinced that we were going to kill them.

To my question, "Quelle nation?" one replied, "Pauvre Radschput!"

We had Indians in front of us, who had come to this godforsaken piece of earth, far across the sea, to get their skulls cracked by Hanoverian fusiliers.

Their dainty bodies were badly battered. At these short distances, rifle bullets have an explosive effect. None of them had received less than two shots. We picked them up and dragged them to our trench. Since they were screaming as if they were on a spit, my men plugged their mouths and threatened them with their fists, which only strengthened their fear. One of them died during the transport. He was taken along anyways, since there was a bounty on every prisoner, dead or alive. The other two tried to win our favor by continually shouting, "Anglais pas bon!" The reason why these people spoke fluent French is not quite clear to me.

In the trench we were received with cheers by the company, which had heard the noise of the battle and received heavy cordon fire, and duly marveled at our spoils. I retreated to our hut with Kius, who immediately took half a dozen pictures, and treated me to some fried eggs to celebrate the day.

Our performance attracted justified attention and was praised in the division's daily agenda. With twenty men we had victoriously resisted a division several times our size, which had already arrived in our rear. Of course, such a success can only be achieved by brilliantly disciplined troops of high moral quality.

I could say to myself with satisfaction that I had caused the enemy's leader a severe disappointment, as well as an early grave, through dominance over the situation and influence over my men.

The enemy's leader had measured our abilities in the same way as is customary in small officer exercises in the garrison; only we had not fired blanks.

If any member of the Indian 1st Hariana Lancers Regiment should read these lines, let him here have my respect, for a troop with leaders as this first lieutenant, against whom I had the honor of fighting, have earned my admiration.

What does Nietzsche say about warriors? "You may only have enemies to hate, but not enemies to despise. You must be proud of your enemy, then the successes of the enemy is also your successes."

The next evening I received orders to reoccupy the field guard, where no one could patrol during the day due to visibility. Kius and I, along with fifty men, formed pincers around the woods and met at the steep slope. There was no sign of the enemy, only from the hollow way, which I had explored with Sergeant Hackmann, a sentry shouted at us, shot a flare and fired his rifle. We made a mental note of this careless young man for our next outing.

There were three corpses at the location where we had fought off the flank attack the previous night. There were two Indians and a white officer with two gold stars on his epaulets, i.e. a first lieutenant. He had been shot in the eye. The bullet had pierced the opposite temple and shattered the rim of his steel helmet, which is now in my collection of such things. His right hand was still holding his club, which was splattered with his own blood, his left hand was clutching a large six-shooter revolver, the cylinder of which only contained two live rounds.

My people looted the fallen. This sight always made me uncomfortable, but I did not interfere, since the things were only exposed to ruin, and aesthetic or moral concerns did not seem to me quite appropriate in this dark meadow over which the raw relentlessness of the battle still hovered.

Over the next few days, a number of corpses hidden in the undergrowth of the copse became noticeable, a sign of the enemy's heavy losses that made remaining in the outpost even less inviting. As soon as I started working my way through the undergrowth, a strange hissing and bubbling sound caught my attention. I stepped closer and came across two corpses that seemed to have eerily come to life as a result of the heat.

On the evening of June 19th, I went out on patrol with little Schultz, ten other men and a light machine gun from the position, which was gradually becoming somewhat oppressive, in order to pay a visit to the sentry who had made himself so noticeable the other day in the hollow way. Schultz went with his men to the right of the hollow way, I went to the left, with the understanding that we would jump to each other's aid if a squad came under fire. We carefully worked our way through grass and gorse, crawling and stopping occasionally to listen.

Suddenly, the racking sound of a round being chambered was heard. We were glued to the ground. Any old patroller will appreciate the series of unpleasant feelings that followed in the next few seconds.

A shot rang out, shattering the overbearing silence. I laid behind a gorse bush and waited. To my right, one of our men was throwing hand grenades into the hollow way.

Suddenly a line of fire sprayed out in front of us. The unbelievably sharp crack of the shots revealed that the gunners were only a few meters away from us. I saw that we had fallen into a nasty trap and called for retreat. Everyone jumped up and ran back in mad haste, while rifle fire on our left also started. In the midst of this unnerving clatter I gave up all hope of a safe return. My subconscious was in constant expectation of a hit. Death was on the hunt.

Somewhere next to us a detachment went after us with a shrill hurrah. Little Schultz later confessed to me that he had thought that a lean Indian swinging a knife was after him and had almost grabbed him by the collar.

At one point I fell to the ground, causing Sergeant Teilengerdes to trip over me. I lost my steel helmet, pistol and hand grenades. Just keep going! Finally we reached the protection of the steep slope and slid down. At the same time Lieutenant Schultz arrived with his men. He told me, while panting, that he had at least chastised the insolent sentry guard with hand grenades. Immediately afterwards two men arrived carrying Fusilier F., who had been shot through both legs. The rest of the men were unharmed.

The greatest misfortune was that the man who had carried the machine gun, a recruit, had tripped over a wounded man and dropped the gun.

While we were still lively debating and planning a second expedition, an artillery barrage began which reminded me exactly of the night of the 12th, also with regard to the hopeless confusion which immediately broke out. I found myself without a weapon on the steep slope alone with the wounded man, who pulled himself forward with both hands, crawled up to me and wailed, "Lieutenant, don't leave me alone!"

I had to leave him, sorry as I was, and take part in the formation of the field guard. I gathered the people in a row of sentry holes at the edge of the forest, and was heartily pleased when the morning dawned without anything special having happened.

At such moments, I was always amazed and moved by the man's faithful confidence in the officer's superiority over the situation.

"Lieutenant, where shall we go?" "Lieutenant, help, I'm wounded!" "Where is the lieutenant?"

In times like these, to be a leader with a clear head holds the most beautiful reward, as cowardice holds its punishment. I have always pitied the coward to whom the battle became a series of hellish torments, while the brave, in their amplified vitality, experienced battle as a series of exciting events.

The following night we found ourselves in the same place with the intention of retrieving our machine gun, but a series of suspicious noises heard as we crept up on them told us that a strong crew must be waiting for us.

It was therefore decided (a point of honor that, like so many others in the war, made us curse inwardly) to recapture the lost weapon by force. We were to attack the enemy postings at 12 o'clock at night, after a three minute artillery preparation, and search for the weapon.

I put on a good face and shot some batteries myself in the afternoon.

At 11 o'clock I found myself again with Schultz, my unlucky comrade, on an eerie piece of earth on which many eventful hours had already blossomed for me. The smell of decay in the sultry air was almost unbearable. We sprinkled the corpses with chlorinated lime, which we had brought with us in sacks. The white spots shone out of the darkness like shrouds.

The enterprise began with the fact that our own machine gun bullets were constantly flying between our legs and slapping into the steep slope. Because of this, a fierce quarrel arose between me and little Schultz, who had set up the rifles himself. We reconciled, however, when Schultz discovered me behind a bush in conversation with a bottle of Burgundy, which I had taken with me to fortify myself for the precarious adventure.

At the appointed time, the first shell roared in. It hit approximately fifty meters behind us. Before we could even wonder about this strange impact, a second one fell next to us on the steep slope and showered us with earth. At this I was not even allowed to curse, because I was the one that communicated the firing location to the artillery.

After this uninspiring introduction, we moved forward, more for the sake of honor than in the hope of success. We were lucky that the guards had apparently left their post, otherwise we would have received a very rude welcome. Unfortunately, we did not find the machine gun this time either.

Since we were relieved the following day by troops from another division, the skirmish came to an end.

We returned to Montbréhain for the time being and marched from there to Cambrai, where we spent almost the entire month of July. The field guard finally fell into enemy hands the night following our relief.

XII

Langemarck

CAMBRAI is a quiet, dreamy Artois town, whose name is linked to many historical memories. Narrow, ancient streets wind around the mighty town hall, weathered city gates and many churches. Massive towers rise from a maze of angular gables. Wide avenues lead to the well-kept city park, which is adorned with a monument to the aviator Blériot.

The inhabitants are quiet, friendly people who live a comfortable bourgeois existence in the large, simple-looking and richly furnished houses. Many people spend their retirement in Cambrai. The town is rightly called "la Ville des millionaires," because just before the war there were over forty millionaires living there.

The Great War brutally tore the quiet rest from its slumber and turned it into a focus of enormous battles. Hasty new lives rumbled across the bumpy pavement and clanked against the small windows behind which anxious faces lurked. Strange fellows drank the lovingly maintained cellars dry, threw themselves into the mighty mahogany beds, and in a state of constant coming and going disturbed the tranquil peace of the private citizens, who now stood together at the entrances of their front doors, in the midst of the transformed environment, whispering to each other in cautious voices concerning seemingly reliable news about the imminent final victory of their countrymen.

The men lived in a barracks, and the officers were housed in the Rue-des-Liniers. This street took on the appearance of a college student neighborhood while we were there; general conversations from the windows, nightly singing, and little romantic adventures were the order of the day.

Every morning we went to drill on the large square near the village of Fontaine, which later became famous. I had a very interesting duty, because Colonel von Oppen had assigned me the training of the storm troops.

My quarters were extremely comfortable; rarely did my hosts, the friendly jeweler couple Plancot-Bourlon, ever let a lunch go by without sending something delicious to my room. We sat together in the evenings over a cup of tea, playing games and chatting. Particularly often, of course, we discussed the hard-to-answer question of why people had to go to war.

During these hours, the good Monsieur Plancot told many tales of the always idle and witty citizens of Cambrai, which in peacetime had set the streets, wine taverns and weekly market into peals of laughter, and which reminded me vividly of Claude Tillier's wonderful Uncle Benjamin.

On July 25th, we said farewell to the precious little town and drove north to Flanders. We had read in the newspapers that an artillery battle had been raging there for weeks, the likes of which have never been seen before in world history.

We were unloaded in Staden under the distant thunder of the canons and marched through the unfamiliar landscape to the Ohndank camp. To the right and left of the dead-straight Chaussée, fertile fields of beets and lush, water-rich meadows surrounded by green hedges. Scattered far and wide were neat farms with low thatched or tiled roofs, on whose walls bundles of tobacco plants were hung to dry. The peasants coming along the way were of the Germanic type and conversed in coarse, homely-sounding language. We spent the afternoon in the gardens of individual homesteads, hidden from the view of enemy planes. From time to time, with a gurgling sound coming from far away, huge caliber shells from naval canons whizzed over our heads and exploded nearby. One shell struck one of the numerous small streams and killed some men from the 91st Regiment while they were bathing.

Towards evening I had to leave with an advance party to the position of the standby battalion in order to prepare the relief and to brief my men. We walked through the Houthulst forest and the village of Kokuit to the reserve battalion and were "put out of step" a few times along the way by heavy shells. In the darkness I heard the voice of a recruit: "The lieutenant never lies down."

"He knows his stuff," he was instructed by an elder. "When the shell is for us, he's the first one to hit the ground!"

The man had seen through my principle, which I always followed. "Take cover only when necessary, but then swiftly." The degree of necessity, however, can only be judged by the experienced warrior, who already has a feeling for the end point of a shell's trajectory before the newcomer even notices the slight, announcing flutter.

Our guides, who did not seem quite sure of their cause, wound their way through an endless "elevated trench." This is the name given to trenches that are not built deep because of the ground water, but are set up above the ground with sandbags and fascines. Then we roamed an eerily mangled forest, from which, according to the tale of the guides, a regimental command post had been driven out by a thousand rounds of 240 mm shells.

After crisscrossing through dense undergrowth, we stood helplessly, abandoned by our guides, on a reedy piece of earth, bordered by marshy swamps, on whose black mirrors the moonlight reflected. There was a continual crashing somewhere nearby, and mud flung upwards and splashed into the water. Finally the unfortunate guide, on whom all our anger was concentrated, returned and claimed to have found the way. He led us astray again, however, to a medical shelter above which a few shells exploded at very short, regular intervals, sending shrapnel and bullets pattering through the branches. The doctor on duty gave us a sensible man to escort us to Mäuseburg, the headquarters of the reserve commander.

I went straight on to the company of 225th Regiment, which was to be relieved by the 2nd Company, and after a long search in the crater area I found some decayed houses, which were inconspicuously reinforced on the inside by reinforced concrete. One of them had been dented by a heavy hit the day before and the crew had been crushed by the collapsing roof, as if in a mousetrap.

I spent the rest of the night in the crowded concrete block of the company commander, a bland front-line pig, who passed the time with his orderlies by means of a bottle of schnapps and a large can of pork, often interrupting this occupation to listen, shaking his head, to the ever-growing artillery fire. Then he used to sigh at the good times in Russia and curse about the fatigue of his regiment. Finally, my eyes fell shut.

The sleep was heavy and agitated; the explosive shells falling in the impenetrable darkness all around the house evoked an indescribable feeling of loneliness and abandonment in the midst of the dead landscape. I involuntarily snuggled up to a man lying next to me on the cot. At a certain point, I was woken up by a strong impact. My men shined a light on the walls, looking for a hole. It turned out that a small caliber shell had burst on the outer wall.

I spent the afternoon of the following day with the battalion commander at the Rattenburg (Rat Castle), since I still had to find out about some important issues. The entire time, 150 mm shells were slamming next to the command post, while the cavalry captain was playing an endless game of skat with his adjutant and the orderly officer, passing around a seltzer bottle full of bad booze. Sometimes he would put down his cards to dispatch an order-bearer or, with a worried expression, put up for discussion the bomb-proofing of our concrete block. Despite his eager rebuttals (mostly wishful thinking on his part) we convinced him that we were no match for a hit from above.

In the evening, the general shelling burned to a furious intensity, in front colorful flares rose in unceasing succession. Dust-covered runners brought word that the enemy was attacking. After weeks of bombardment, the infantry battle was launched.

Returning to the stand of the company commander, I waited for the arrival of the 2nd Company, which appeared at 4 a.m. during a lively fire raid. I immediately took over my platoon and led it to its place, a concrete building covered by the debris of a destroyed house, which lay unspeakably abandoned in the middle of a huge crater field of horrible desolation.

At 6 a.m. the dense Flanders fog lifted, giving us a view of our eerie surroundings. Immediately thereafter, hanging close above the ground, a swarm of enemy planes appeared and, emitting siren signals, scoured the pounded terrain while scattered infantrymen sought to hide in shell holes.

Half an hour later, a terrible bombardment began, engulfing our island of refuge like a tsunami. The forest of impacts around us condensed into a swirling wall. We huddled together, expecting at any moment the blaring hit that would sweep us away, along with the concrete blocks, and flatten our shelter into this crater-riddled desert that surrounds us.

The entire day passed this way, switching between tremendous bursts of fire and longer breaks to get ourselves prepared.

In the evening, an exhausted orderly appeared and handed me an order from which I learned that the 1st, 3rd and 4th Companies were to counterattack at 10:50 a.m., the 2nd Company was to await its relief and swarm into the front line. In order to be able to face the next few hours with strength, I laid down, not suspecting that my brother Fritz, whom I thought was still in Hanover, was advancing with an assault group of the 3rd Company, crossing the fire canopy very close to my hut.

My sleep was disturbed for a long time by the wailing of a wounded man, whom two Saxons had left behind, lost in the craters and who had fallen asleep from extreme fatigue. When they woke up the next morning, their comrade was dead. They carried him to the nearest shell hole, covered him with a few shovels of earth, and departed, leaving behind one of the countless lonely, unknown graves of the war.

I woke up from my deep slumber at 11 o'clock, washed in my steel helmet, and sent for orders to the company commander, who, to my astonishment, had already departed without even notifying me or the platoon.

The consequences of this were that officers of foreign armies were sent into the infantry battle at the head of companies only because of their seniority. Such considerations of rank may be applied, if one does not think one can do without them, as long as no human lives are in question.

We cursed about it many times in the dugout and behind the cup, but only among ourselves. It was more pleasant to storm against Fort

Douaumont than against this ancient hereditary evil. The Frederician spirit in high honor, but wigs, braids and rank on chamber to the blunderbusses of 1806, if it should go off again.

While I was still sitting on my cot cursing and wondering what to do, an orderly from the battalion appeared and handed me the order to take over the 8th Company immediately.

I learned that the counterattack of the 1st Battalion had collapsed the previous night with heavy losses, and that the remnants had taken up a defensive position in a small patch of forest in front of us, the so-called Dobschütz Forest, as well as to the right and left of it. The 8th Company had been ordered to swarm into the copse for reinforcements, but had been destroyed in the intervening terrain in a barrage of heavy casualties. Since the company commander, First Lieutenant Büdingen, had also fallen, it was up to me to bring the company back into combat.

After bidding farewell to my orphaned platoon, I set off with the orderly across the shrapnel strewn wasteland. A despairing voice halted our stooped run for a moment. In the distance, a figure with a bleeding stump for an arm, half sticking out of a crater, beckoned. We pointed back to our abandoned hut and hurried on.

I found the 8th Company to be a demoralized bunch, squatting behind a row of concrete blocks, declaring it impossible to make another move against the wall of heavy impacts separating us from the Dobschütz Forest. Seven men called in sick.

On the other hand, I only had the proof ad oculos left. I ordered them to follow me and jumped into the middle of the fire. After uttering only a few sentences a shell, which fortunately threw its column of earth up quite steeply, showered me with dirt clumps and hurled me into the nearest crater. I soon realized, however, that the fury of the fire was diminishing farther ahead. After making my way forward another two hundred meters, I looked around. The area was deserted.

Finally, two men emerged from clouds of smoke and dust, then another, then two more. With these five men, I happily reached my destination.

In a half-shattered concrete block sat Lieutenant Sandvoß, leader of the 3rd Company, and little Schultz along with three heavy machine guns. I was received with a loud hello and a sip of cognac, then they explained the situation, which was not very pleasant. Close in front of us sat the English, but we had no contact with either the right or left of our position.

Sandvoß asked me abruptly if I had heard anything from my brother. You can imagine my feelings when I learned that he had been in yesterday's storm and was missing.

Immediately a man came and told me that my brother was wounded and laying in a nearby dugout, pointing to a desolate log cabin covered with uprooted trees. I hurried across a clearing under well-aimed rifle fire and entered the cabin. What a reunion! My brother was in a room filled with the smell of corpses amid a crowd of groaning, severely wounded men. He was in a sorry state. Two shrapnel bullets had hit him during the storm, one had pierced his lung, the other had shattered his right humeral joint. His eyes glowed with fever; he could move, speak and breathe only with difficulty. We squeezed each other's hand and recounted our respective adventures.

It was clear to me that he could not stay in this place, because at any moment the English could storm, or a shell could finish off the already heavily damaged concrete block. The best brotherly service was to bring him back immediately. Despite Sandvoß's reluctance to weaken our fighting strength, I gave the five men who had come with me the order to take my brother to the "Kolumbusei" medical shelter and from there to bring more men to rescue the other wounded in the cabin. We knotted him in a tent and put a long pole through it, then two men took him on their shoulders. Another handshake, then the sad procession started to move.

From the edge of the copse, I watched the swinging load wind its way through a forest of earthen columns, as tall as the trees, raised by falling shells.

After skirmishing a little more, from the trenches at the edge of the small forest, with the slowly advancing English, I spent the night with my men and a machine-gun operator among the rubble of the concrete block. Nearby, explosive shells of an extraordinarily large caliber were constantly thundering down all around us, one of which almost killed me that evening. Towards morning, the machine-gunner suddenly rattled off as dark figures approached. It was a liaison patrol of the 76th Infantry Regiment, from which he shot down one man. Such mistakes were frequent in those days, without much attention being paid to them.

At 6 o'clock in the morning we were relieved by parts of the 9th Company, who passed me the order to occupy the Rattenburg with my men. On the way there I was incapacitated by a shrapnel shot.

The Rattenburg presented itself to us as a shot-up, reinforced concrete-brick house, located near the marshy bed of the Steenbach, which probably deserved its name. Quite demoralized, we threw ourselves on the straw-covered cots until a plentiful lunch and the encouraging pipe of tobacco afterwards got us back on our feet.

In the early afternoon hours a continuous shelling with heavy calibers began. From 6 to 8 o'clock one explosion followed the other; often the building was shaken by the terrible impacts of nearby duds and threatened to collapse. When the fire died down in the evening, I stalked to the "Kolumbusei" medical shelter and inquired about my brother from the doctor, who was examining the horribly mangled leg of a dying man. I was pleased to hear that he had been delivered to the rear in relatively good condition.

At a late hour, my troop of food carriers appeared and brought the small company, which had dwindled to twenty men, hot food, canned meat, coffee, bread, tobacco and schnapps. We ate heartily and, without any annoying distinction of rank, finished off the bottle of "ninety-eight proof alcohol." Then we gave ourselves up to sleep, which was abundantly disturbed by swarms of mosquitoes coming from the bottom of the stream, shells and intermittent gas attacks.

As a result, I slept so soundly the next morning that my men had to wake me up after hours of heavy bombardment. They reported that men were constantly coming back from the front, claiming that the front line had been evacuated and that the enemy was advancing.

Following the old soldier's maxim: "A good breakfast keeps body and soul together," I first fortified myself, lit a pipe, and then went to see what was going on outside.

I had only a modest overview, since the whole area was shrouded in dense smoke. The artillery fire became more violent by the minute and soon reached that climax at which the nervous excitement, incapable of any further increase, turns into an almost amusing indifference. Continuous showers of earth clods pelted our roof, twice the house itself was hit. Incendiary shells threw up heavy, milk-white clouds from which fiery drops trickled to earth. A piece of this burning mass splashed on a stone in front of my feet and continued to burn for several minutes. Deceleration shells burrowed into the ground, kicking up shallow bells of earth. Clouds of gas and fog crept slowly across the battlefield. In front of us, rifle and machine-gun fire rang out, a sign that the enemy was getting close.

Down in the Steenbach valley, a platoon strode through the shifting forest of high-splashing mud geysers. I recognized the battalion commander, Captain von Brixen, who was leaning on two medics with a bandaged arm, and hurried towards him. He hastily called out to me that the enemy was advancing and warned me not to linger any longer without cover.

Soon the first infantry shells started clapping into the surrounding craters or pounding against the remains of the wall. More and more fleeing figures disappeared behind us in the haze, while frenzied rifle fire testified to the fierce defense of those holding strong in front.

It was time to act. I decided to defend the Rattenburg and made it clear to the people, some of whom were pulling worried faces, that I was not even remotely thinking about retreating. The crew was spread out behind embrasures, and our only machine gun was placed in a window opening. A crater was designated as a dressing station, and a medic, who immediately found plenty of work, was placed inside. I, too, picked up a rifle lying on the ground and hung a belt of cartridges around my neck.

Since my little group was very small, I tried to reinforce it with the numerous men wandering around without a guide. Most of them willingly followed our calls, glad to be able to join, while others, abandoned by their nerves, hurried on after a moment's pause. In such cases, any tender consideration ceases.

I shouted to my men who were standing in front of me in the shelter of the house, and a few shots were fired. Magnetically attracted by the muzzles of the rifles, these shirkers, unavoidable in any battle, slowly approached, although one could see from their expressions how reluctant they were to keep us company. An orderly, well known to me, tried to fall back, giving me all kinds of excuses, but I did not let him go.

"But I don't have a rifle!"

"Then you wait until someone with a rifle is shot dead!"

During one last enormous burst of fire, during which a dilapidated house was hit several times and the chunks of bricks flew high in the air and landed on our steel helmets. I was thrown to the ground in the flash of a terrible blow. To the astonishment of my men, I pulled myself up, unharmed.

After this final mighty storm, things quieted down. The fire passed over us and stopped at the road Langemarck-Bixschoote. We were not comfortable with it. So far we had not seen the forest for the trees; the danger had come upon us in such a tremendous and multiform way that we could not deal with it. After the storm had roared over us, everyone found time to prepare for what would inevitably come.

And it came. The guns in front of us fell silent. The defenders were finished. Out of the smoke emerged a dense line of riflemen. My men fired, crouching behind the rubble, the machine gun cracking. As if wiped away, the attackers disappeared into the craters, trapping us with their fire. To the right and left, strong detachments advanced. Soon we were surrounded by a ring of riflemen.

The situation was hopeless; there was no point in sacrificing the crew. I gave the order to retreat. It was difficult to get the men up who were so engaged in the fight.

Taking advantage of a cloud of smoke lying in the bottom, we managed to escape without being noticed. I was the last to leave the small fortress, supporting Lieutenant Höhlemann, who was bleeding from a severe head wound and making light of his awkwardness with a few jokes.

Crossing the road, we encountered the 2nd Company, which had been sent forward for reinforcements. After a short consultation we decided to stay and await the enemy. Here, too, we had to force the men from other units, who wanted to continue retreating on their own authority, to stay. Especially artillerymen, signalmen, telephonists, etc., could only be forcibly persuaded that in such circumstances they, too, should take up their rifles and join the others. With pleas, orders and rifle butt blows, I soon established order with the help of Kius and some other cool headed men.

Then we sat down in an indicated trench and had breakfast. Kius pulled out his inseparable apparatus and took some photographs. We noticed some movement to the left in front of us at the exit of Langemarck. Our men fired at the figures wandering about. Soon a non-commissioned officer appeared and reported that a company of Fusiliers had nestled along the road and had suffered casualties from our fire.

I then had them advance to their height under heavy rifle fire. Some men fell, Lieutenant Bartmer of the 2nd Company was seriously wounded. Kius remained at my side, finishing his sandwich as we proceeded. When we had occupied the road from which the terrain sloped down to the Steenbach, we noticed that the English were about to do the same. The first khaki colored figures were already starting to appear within twenty meters of our position. As far as the eye could see, the foreland was filled with lines of riflemen and columns of ranks. They were also beginning to swarm around the Rattenburg.

We energetically took advantage of our element of surprise and immediately fired on them. At the Steenbach, a whole row of them collapsed. One of them had a roll of wire on his back from which he was unwinding a line. Others jumped back and forth like rabbits, while next to them the dust clouds of our bullets whirled up. A strapping Fusilier of the 8th Company, with the utmost calm, laid his rifle on a splintered tree stump and shot down four opponents in succession. The rest crawled into shell craters to hide there until dark. We had cleaned up well.

Around 11 a.m., a cockade-adorned aircraft swooped down on us and were immediately driven away by a lively fire on our part, to which they responded from above.

Immediately after the occupation of the road I had written a report to the regiment asking for support. In the afternoon infantry platoons, sappers and machine guns came to reinforce. According to the tactics of Old Fritzen, all the reinforcements were put into the crowded front line. Now and then, the English would cut down some careless men crossing the road.

Around 4 o'clock a very unpleasant shrapnel shooting began. The batteries were hurled as close as possible to the road. It was clear to me that the airmen had established our new line of resistance and that we still had some difficult hours ahead of us.

In fact, a tremendous shelling with light and heavy shells soon began. We laid close together in the crowded, dead-straight trench. The fire danced before our eyes, twigs and clods of clay whistled down on us. To my left, a blaze of fire flared up, leaving behind a white, suffocating smoke. I crawled on all fours to the man next to me. He was no longer moving. Blood oozed from many wounds struck by narrow, jagged splinters. Further to the right, heavy casualties were also occurring.

After half an hour, it became quiet. We diligently dug deep holes in the shallow hollow of the trench, in order to at least have protection against splinters in case of a second raid. Our spades dug up rifles, belt gear and cartridge cases from 1914, a sure sign that this ground was not drinking blood for the first time. During the twilight we were thoroughly considered once again by the airmen. I squatted next to Lieutenant Kius in a hole that had cost us many a callus. The ground rolled like the deck of a ship under continual impacts, falling closer and closer. We were prepared for the end.

The steel helmet pressed into my forehead, I chewed my pipe and stared at the road, whose stones were spraying sparks under bursting chunks of iron. The strangest thoughts flashed through my mind. Thus I occupied myself vividly with a trash French novel "le vautour de la Sierra," which had fallen into my hands in Cambrai. Several times I murmured a word of Ariost: "A great heart feels no horror before death, whenever it comes, so long as it is glorious!" Today it tastes a bit like theater to me; at that time it helped me to keep my composure. When the shells gave the ear some rest, I heard fragments of the beautiful song of the "Black Whale at Ascalon" next to me and thought my friend Kius had gone mad. Everyone has his own way of tranquilizing his nerves.

At the end of the shelling, a large splinter flew against my hand. Kius shone his flashlight. We noticed a shallow scratch.

Hours like the one we just experienced were without a doubt the most terrible of the entire war.

You cower huddled in your lonely hole in the ground and feel yourself abandoned to a merciless, blind will of destruction. With horror you suspect that all your intelligence, your abilities, your mental and physical advantages have become an insignificant, ridiculous thing. While you are thinking this, the iron block may have already started its hurtling ride, which will crush you into a formless nothingness. Your uneasiness is concentrated on your hearing, which tries to distinguish the approaching flutter of the death-bringer from the multitude of noises.

It is dark at the same time. You have to draw all the strength from yourself to endure. You can't even stand up and light a cigarette with a smug smile, lifting yourself up at the admiring glances of your comrades. You're not encouraged by your friend next to you who, tucked in the hole, is peering over the edge through the scope of a rifle. You know that if it hits you, no rooster will crow about it.

Yes, why don't you jump up and rush into the night until you collapse in a safe bush like an exhausted animal? Why do you still persevere, you and your brave men? No superior sees you.

And yet someone is watching you. Perhaps unconscious to yourself, the moral man is at work in you, binding you to the place by two powerful factors: duty and honor. You know that you are placed in this place to fight and that a whole nation trusts you to do your thing. You believe that if you leave your place now, you will be a coward before yourself, a rascal who will blush later at every word of praise. You grit your teeth and stay.

That evening, everyone on the dark Flanders road who remained in their hole persevered. One could see that the leader and crew stood up in a heroic spirit.

Duty and honor must be the cornerstones of every army. And the officer, as the foremost fighter, must be instilled with a sense of maximum duty and honor. For this you need suitable material and certain forms. This becomes quite clear to one only in war.

After midnight it began to trickle; patrols of a regiment that had in the meantime swarmed in and advanced to the Steenbach found only mud-filled craters. The enemy had retreated behind the creek.

Exhausted by the exertions of this tremendous day, we sat down in our holes, except for the men separated into sentry posts. I pulled the tattered coat of my dead neighbor over my head and fell into a restless sleep. At the time of dawn I was awakened by a strange cold sensation and discovered that I was in a deplorable position. It was raining in torrents, and the rivulets of the road were pouring into the depths of my sitting hole. I built a small dam and scooped out my resting place with the cookware lid. As a result of the constant increase in the amount of water, I had to put one crest after another on my earthwork, until finally the weak structure gave way to the growing pressure, and a dirty, gurgling stream filled my hole to the top. While I struggled to fish a pistol and steel helmet out of the mud, tobacco and foodstuffs floated along the ditch of the Chaussée, whose other inhabitants had fared similarly. Shivering and freezing, without a dry thread on our bodies, we stood in the muddy street, aware that we would be completely exposed to the next shelling. It was a miserable situation. I made the observation here that no artillery fire is able to break the resistance of man as thoroughly as the wet and cold.

For the further course of the battle this water issue was actually a real godsend, because, in the first, most crucial days, the English offensive had to come to a complete standstill because of it. The enemy had to overcome the swampy crater zone with his artillery, while we were able to roll in our ammunition on intact roads, via the Chaussée.

At 11 o'clock, when despair had already seized us, a guardian angel appeared, in the form of a dispatch runner, who brought the order that the regiment should assemble in Kokuit.

On the way we saw how difficult the connection to the front must have been on the day of the attack. The streets were littered with men and horses. In addition to a number of men smashed beyond recognition, twelve horribly mutilated horses laid in a heap.

On a meadow drenched by rain, over which isolated shrapnel bombs were bursting with milky-white clouds, the remnants of the regiment gathered. We were shocked by the sight of this small band of soldiers, no more numerous than a company's personnel, gathered around a couple of officers. What losses! From two battalions almost all were officers and enlisted men. The survivors stood gloomily in the pouring rain until quarters were arranged. We dried ourselves in a wooden barrack, gathered around a glowing stove, and with a hearty breakfast regained our courage to live. Human nature is simply indestructible.

Towards evening shells hit the village. One of the barracks was hit and a number of people from the 3rd Company were killed. Despite the shelling, we soon laid down with the only hope of not being thrown back out into the rain for a counterattack or a sudden defense.

At 3 o'clock in the morning the order came for the final disengagement. We marched along the road to Staden, which was strewn with corpses and shot-up cars. Around the edge of a huge impact crater laid twelve dead. Staden, which had been so lively when we arrived, already had many shot-up houses. The desolate marketplace was strewn with discarded household goods. A family left the town with us, dragging a cow behind them as their only possession. The man had a stilt, the woman held a crying child by the hand. The chaotic noise in the back increased the sadness of the picture.

The remnants of the 2nd Battalion were housed in a lonely courtyard hidden behind thick hedges in the midst of tall, lush fields. There I was put in charge of the 7th Company, with whom I was to share joys and sorrows until the end of the war.

We spent the evening sitting in front of the fireplace lined with old tiles, fortified ourselves by a stiff grog and listened to the reviving thunder of the battle. From the army report of a new newspaper the sentence jumped into my eyes: "We succeeded in stopping the enemy at the Steenbach line."

It was strange to feel that our seemingly confused actions in the dark of night had achieved world-historical significance. We had made a good contribution to bringing the enemy offensive, which had begun with such a tremendous force, to a standstill.

We went to the hayloft to rest. Despite the copious nightcap, most of the sleepers dreamed, tossing and turning, as if they had to fight through the Battle of Flanders all over again.

On July 3rd, richly supplied with cattle and crops of the deserted region, we set out for the train station of the nearby town of Gits. In the station pub the whole shrunken battalion drank coffee again in a brilliant mood, which two coarse Flemish waitresses seasoned with very spicy expressions for general amusement. The men especially enjoyed using "du" to treat everyone, including the officers, according to the custom of the country.

* * *

After a few days I received a letter from my brother in a military hospital in Gelsenkirchen. He wrote that he would probably keep a stiff arm and a rickety lung.

I take the following lines from his diary, which supplement my report and vividly reflect the impressions of a newcomer thrown into the hell of an immense battle:

"'Fall in for the storm!' The face of my platoon leader and vice sergeant Schnell bent over the entrance to the small leaf and board covered hut where we had been lying for hours smoking and eating. The three people next to me finished their conversation and gathered themselves up, cursing. I rose, buckled up, tightened my steel helmet and stepped out into the twilight.

It was foggy and cool. The picture had changed in the meantime. The shellfire had faded and now weighed, with dull thundering, on other parts of the vast battlefield. Airplanes roared through the air, reassuring the anxiously peering eye with their great iron crosses.

I ran once more to a well that, strangely, had preserved itself, remaining visible among the rubble and debris. I pulled up the bucket, drank, and filled my canteen.

The men of the company came in platoons. I hurriedly hooked four hand grenades into my belt and went to my group, of which two men were missing. I barely had time to write down the names when everything started to move. In single file, the platoons moved through the crater terrain, bypassing tree trunks, squeezing by hedges, diving into depths, and winding, clanking and rumbling, toward the enemy.

I was clearly aware of my mission. The 2nd Battalion of our regiment and a battalion of the neighboring regiment had orders to repel English divisions that had pushed across the channel. I was to remain in front with my group and intercept the counterattack.

While I was thinking all this over again, my gaze met the pale, determined face of a young sergeant. 'Bachmann,' I thought, although I did not know him. It was a comrade, a Fahnenjunker-Unteroffizier, also with the Sandvoß Company. I lost sight of him and gazed in amazement at the landscape that had suddenly developed before our eyes.

We had arrived in front of the ruins of a village. Out of the terribly scarred plain of Flanders, black and splintered, rose the branchless stumps of individual trees, remnants of a great forest. Monstrous clouds of smoke floated through the air, blanketing the sky with gloomy, heavy clouds. Above the bare earth, so ruthlessly torn and torn again, asphyxiating yellow and brown gases smoldered, drifting lazily.

Gas readiness was ordered. At that moment, abruptly, a tremendous fire started. Earth sprang up in hissing fountains, and storms of steel swept the land like a rain shower. For a moment everyone stood frozen. Then everything fell apart as if in a frenzy. Once again I heard the incomprehensible voice of our battalion commander, Rittmeister Böckelmann.

My men had disappeared, I was in another platoon and pushed with the others for the ruins of a village that the relentless shells had shaved to the foundation walls. We tore out the gas masks.

In an instant, a terrific machine-gun fire began. Everyone threw themselves on the ground. To my left, Lieutenant Ehlers knelt, next to him a sergeant laid peering. In front of us a wall of fire flickered yellow, detonation followed detonation; remnants of houses, a shower of clods of earth, pieces of bricks and steel splinters hailed down on us and struck the steel helmets sending bright sparks. I stared into this glowing infernal cauldron.

I realized that our attack had been aborted by the violence of that barrage. Twice, at short intervals, a colossal explosion swallowed up all the noise. They were the bursts of two shells of the highest caliber. Whole fields of debris flew into the air, whirled around and crashed down with a hellish patter.

At a shouted request from Ehlers, I looked to my right. He raised his left hand, making a sign to fall back, and jumped up. I wearily got to my feet and ran after him. My feet still burned like fire from the previous night, but the blood had been absorbed by my stockings and the stinging pain had subsided.

I had not taken twenty steps when, emerging from a crater, I was blinded by the burning light of a shrapnel bursting not ten steps in front of me at a height of three meters. I felt two dull blows against my chest and shoulder. Automatically the rifle fell from my hand, I collapsed, head back, and rolled back into the crater. In a blur, I could still hear the voice of Ehler, who shouted as he ran past, 'He's been hit.'

Ehler would not see the following day. The advance failed and he was killed while jumping back with all his companions. A shot through the back of the head put an end to the life of this brave officer.

When I regained consciousness after a long faint, it had become quiet. I tried to sit up, but felt a sharp pain in my right shoulder, which every movement of the arm intensified. Breathing was short and intermittent, my lungs were unable to take in enough air. 'Bruised lung and shoulder,' I thought, throwing away the assault pack, the belt and, in a state of complete apathy, the gas mask as well. I kept the steel helmet on and hung the canteen on the waist hook.

After five steps, I remained motionless in another crater. After perhaps an hour, I tried to crawl away for the second time, since the field was again showered with light drum fires. This attempt also failed; I lost my canteen and sank into an endless exhaustion, from which, after a long time, the feeling of a burning thirst woke me up.

It began to rain softly. With the steel helmet I managed to collect a little dirty water. I had lost all orientation. A thunderstorm was coming, its thunderclaps drowned out by the incipient noise of a new drumfire. I pressed myself against the crater wall. A lump of clay hit my shoulder, heavy splinters swept over my head. Gradually, I also lost any sense of time.

Once two men appeared, setting off in long leaps across the field. I called to them; they disappeared without hearing me like shadows in the mists. At last three men came straight toward me. I recognized the one in the middle as the sergeant from the day before. They took me to a small hut that was nearby, crammed with wounded being tended by two medics. I had been in the crater for thirteen hours.

In a corner of the hut I recognized Bachmann, who, biting his pain, held his shot knee convulsively. We talked brokenly; sometimes, when someone nudged him, he moaned softly.

The tremendous fire continued its work. Shell after shell hit next to us, often showering the roof with sand and earth. I was bandaged, given a new gas mask, a loaf of bread with coarse red jam and a little water. The medic took care of us like a father would his sons.

The English began to advance. They approached by leaps and bounds and disappeared into the craters, as I concluded from the fearful exclamations heard outside.

Then my company commander, Lieutenant Sandvoß, entered, asked me if I could leave and disappeared, recalled by an orderly. Immediately after that I heard his commanding voice, machine guns were repositioned and began to hack.

Suddenly a young officer, with the iron cross on his chest, rushed in, smeared with clay from his shoes to his steel helmet. It was my brother, Ernst, who had been pronounced dead the day before. We greeted each other with a strange, slightly emotional smile. After a few minutes he left me and brought in the last five people of his company. I was laid on a canvas and carried off the battlefield amid the thunder of guns and falling shells."

XIII

Regniéville

ON August 4, 1917, we arrived by train at the famous village of Mars-la-Tour. The 7th and 8th Companies set up their quarters in Doncourt, where we lived a quiet life for a few days. Only the scanty rations brought me into some conflict. It was strictly forbidden to forage in the fields, nevertheless, almost every morning the military police reported to me some men they had encountered while clearing potatoes at night and whose punishment I could not avoid.

On August 9th the company was inspected by the division commander, Major General von Busse, who commended us for good conduct in action. The next afternoon we were loaded and drove to the vicinity of Thiaucourt. From there we marched immediately to our new position, which stretched along the wooded heights of the Côte Lorraine opposite the shot-up village of Regniéville, familiar to us from many a day's command. On the first morning I inspected my section, which seemed to me to be rather long for a company and consisted of a confusing tangle of half-ruined trenches. The front line was also leveled in many places by the heavy, three-winged shells common in this position. My shelter is located about a hundred meters back in the so-called Traffic Trench, near the road leading out of Regniéville. For the first time in a long time we were facing Frenchmen.

The walls of the trench were made of limestone, a material that was much more resistant to weathering than the usual clay soil. In some places, the trench was even carefully walled and over long stretches the bottom was concreted, so that even the heaviest downpours could easily run off. The reddish-white rock was teeming with fossils. Each time I walked the trench, I returned to my shelter with bags full of shells, starfish, and ammonium horns.

My shelter was deep and damp. It had a characteristic that gave me little pleasure, despite the fact that I am otherwise a passionate entomologist. Namely, instead of the usual aphids, the much more mobile relatives occurred in this area. These two species are apparently in the same hostile relationship to each other as the Norway rat and the house rat. Here not even the usual change of linen helped, because the jumping parasites lurked treacherously in the straw of the storage place. The sleeper, driven to despair, finally tore out his blankets and was able to talk to Mephisto:

> I shake the old fluff once more,
> Another one flutters out here and there,
> Up, around in a hundred thousand corners,
> Hasten to hide your sweetheart.

Even the food left much to be desired. Apart from the thin midday soup, there was only a third of bread with a ridiculously small garnish, which mostly consisted of half-rotten jam. Half of it was eaten up every time by a fat rat, which I often chased in vain.

The reserve and rest companies stayed in romantically situated log settlements hidden deep in the woods. I particularly liked my quarters in the reserve position, the "Log Camp," which was positioned in a blind spot on the slope of a narrow forest ravine. I lived there in a tiny little hut half built into the slope, densely enclosed by hazelnut bushes and cornel cherries. The window offered a view of the opposite wooded ridge and a narrow creek-strewn meadow strip at the bottom. A collection of bottles of all kinds piled up on the back wall revealed that more than one hermit must have spent many contemplative hours here, and I too tried not to neglect the venerable custom of the place. In the evening, when the mists rose from the ground, mingling with the heavy white smoke of my wood fire, I squatted with the door open in the first twilight between the fresh autumn air and the warmth of the fire, only one drink seemed suitable: half red wine and half egg cognac in a bulbous glass. These intimate celebrations also made me comfortable with the fact that a senior gentleman who had come from the replacement battalion had taken over my company, and I was back on boring trench duty as platoon leader. I tried to avoid the endless hours of guard duty by frequent patrols according to my old habit.

On August 24th, the gallant Rittmeister Böckelmann was wounded by shrapnel. He was the third battalion commander the regiment lost in a short time. On the 29th, I paid a visit to the enemy line with Corporal Kloppmann, the most efficient member of the 7th Company. We crawled toward a gap in the enemy obstacle that Kloppmann had cut the night before. To our unpleasant surprise, the wire was mended; nevertheless, we cut it again, making a lot of noise, and descended into the trench. We crouched down behind the nearest parapet and listened. After a quarter of an hour's lurking, we crept on, following a telephone wire that ended at a bayonet stuck in the ground. We found the position blocked by wire several times and once by a latticed door, but unoccupied. After looking at everything carefully, we went back the same way, carefully bracing the gap again so as not to give away our visit.

The next evening, Kloppmann took another look around the spot, but was met with rifle shots and lemon shaped hand grenades, the so-called "duck eggs." One of them landed right next to his head, which he had pressed to the ground, without killing him—he managed to take to his heels quickly enough to escape the blast.

On September 10th, I went from the log camp to the regimental command post to file for leave. "I have already thought of you," Colonel von Oppen replied to me, "but the regiment must make a reconnaissance, of which you are to take the lead. Pick out suitable men and practice with them down at the Souloeuvre camp."

We were to infiltrate the enemy trench in two places and try to take a few prisoners. The patrol was split into three parts, two assault squads and a security squad, which was to occupy the first line and cover our backs. I took the lead of the left squad, the right one was given to Lieutenant von Kienitz. The group was only composed of volunteers; some of the supernumeraries almost cried when I had to turn them away. My squad, including myself, consisted of fourteen men, among them Ensign von Zglinitzky, Sergeant Kloppmann,

Sergeant Mevius, Sergeant Dujesiefken and two sappers. The greatest daredevils of the 2nd Battalion had come together.

For ten days we trained ourselves in throwing hand grenades and carried out our enterprise on a storm-work that was modeled on reality. It was a miracle that, with the overzealousness of my men, I only had three wounded by shrapnel before the operation even began. Apart from this storm-work we were dispensed from any other service, so on the afternoon of September 22nd, as master of a feral but serviceable band of men, I moved to the second position where we were to be quartered for the night.

In the evening, von Kienitz and I made a pilgrimage through the dark forest to the battalion command post, since we had been invited by the battalion commander, Rittmeister Schumacher, to a last meal. Then we laid down to sleep in our shelter. It is a strange feeling when you know that you will have to fight a battle to the death the next morning and listen to yourself for a while before falling asleep.

At 3 o'clock we were awakened, got up, washed and had breakfast prepared. I was immediately in a lot of trouble, because my lad had completely over-salted the fried eggs that I wanted to have to fortify myself and celebrate the day.

We pushed the plates aside and talked through, for the hundredth time, all the details and scenarios we could come up with. In between, we offered each other cherry brandies while von Kienitz cracked some age-old jokes. Twenty minutes to five, we gathered the people and led them into the front line support bunkers. Gaps had already been cut in the wire and long arrows drawn with lime powder pointed to our attack points. We parted with a handshake and awaited what was to come.

I was completely dressed: In front of my chest I had two sandbags with four stick grenades in each bag, the left one held percussion grenades, the right one held timed grenades; in my right coat pocket a Luger P08 pistol tied to a long strap; in my right pants pocket a small Mauser 1914 pistol; in my left coat pocket five duck egg grenades; in the left pants pocket a phosphorescent compass and a whistle. On my belt a snap hook to pull off the hand grenades, a dagger and wire cutters. In my inner breast pocket was a stuffed wallet and my home address, in the back coat pocket was a flat bottle full of cherry brandy. We had taken off our epaulettes and Gibraltar ribbon so as not to give the enemy any information about our origins. As a sign of recognition, we wore a white armband.

At four minutes to five, diversionary fire began from the left rear division. At 5 o'clock our artillery and shell fire broke out abruptly. I was standing with Sergeant Kloppmann in front of the tunnel entrance smoking a last cigar; however, we were forced to take cover several times because a large number of the shots fired by our side fell with too short a trajectory. With our watches in our hands we counted the minutes.

At 5:05 sharp we moved out of the tunnel and through the obstacle on the prepared paths. I ran ahead, raising a hand grenade, and also saw the right patrol rushing forward in the first light of day. The enemy entanglement was weak; I jumped over it in two leaps, but tripped over a wire roller drawn behind it and fell into a crater, from which NCOs Kloppmann and Mevius pulled me out. "Run!" We jumped into the first line without encountering resistance, while on the right a hand grenade fight began. Without caring, we passed over the sandbag barricade blocking the next trench and jumped forward from crater to crater until we reached two lines of Spanish horsemen separating us from the second line. Since the second line was completely deserted and offered no possibility of taking prisoners, we continued our advance through a barricaded running trench.

At the junction with the third line, a smoldering cigarette was found on the ground in front of me, which indicated that the enemy was very close. I signaled to my men, gripped the hand grenade tighter and carefully crept forward through the well-built trench, against the walls of which leaned numerous abandoned rifles. In such situations the memory unconsciously registers even the most trivial things. Thus, at the trench cross, an image of a cooking pot with a spoon in it imprinted itself on my mind. This observation saved my life twenty minutes later.

Suddenly, shadowy figures disappeared in front of us. We ran after them and came to a dead end, in the wall of which a tunnel entrance had been bored. I stood in front of it and yelled, "Montez!"

In response, a hand grenade was tossed out. It exploded at the level of my head against the opposite wall, shredded my silk cap, wounded my left hand in several places and lopped off the tip of my little finger. The engineer sergeant standing next to me had his nose pierced. We retreated a few steps and bombarded the dangerous place with hand grenades. One of our overzealous men hurled an incendiary bomb into the entrance, making any further attack impossible. We turned back and pursued the third line in the opposite direction, finally catching an enemy. Discarded weapons and pieces of equipment were scattered everywhere. The question, "Where might the owners of all these guns be?" rose ever more eerily in our minds, but we hurried resolutely on through the foggy, barren trenches with hand grenades at the ready and pistols pointed.

Our path from there on became clear to me only upon later reflection. Without realizing it, we turned into a third running trench and, already in the middle of our own cordon fire, approached the fourth line. Every now and then we tore open one of the crates built into the walls and took a hand grenade as a souvenir.

After we had run through cross and transverse trenches a few times, no one knew where we were and in which direction the German positions were. Gradually everyone became agitated. The needles of the phosphorescent compasses danced in our trembling hands, and in searching for the North Star, all our schooling failed us in the excitement. The babbling voices in nearby trenches revealed that the enemy had recovered from the initial surprise. It wouldn't be long until they figure out our position.

After we had turned back once again, I was the last to go and suddenly saw the muzzle of a machine gun swinging back and forth in front of me above a sandbag. I jumped towards it, stumbling over a dead Frenchman, and caught sight of Sergeant Kloppmann and Ensign von Zglinitzky, who were busy with their rifles, while Fusilier Haller was rummaging with bloody hands through a corpse for papers. We fiddled with the machine gun in a feverish panic, not caring about the surroundings, in order to at least bring something back. I tried to loosen the retaining screws; another pinched off the magazine belt with the wire cutters; finally we just grabbed the thing, with tripod intact, and took it with us. At that moment, from a parallel trench in the direction where we thought our trench was, a voice rang out, "Qu'est ce qu'il y a," and a black ball, silhouetted indistinctly against the dawning sky, flew toward us. "Look out!" There was a flash between Mevius and me; a splinter went into Mevius' hand. We scattered on all sides, getting entangled deeper and deeper in the trench system. Only the pioneer sergeant and Mevius were still with me. Our only luck was the fearful French, who still did not dare to come out of their holes. However, it would only be a matter of minutes before we encounter a stronger division that would have been delighted to finish us off. There was no mood of pardon in the air.

As soon as I had already given up all hope of getting out of this cauldron in one piece, a sudden cry of joy escaped me. My gaze had fallen on the cooking pot with the spoon sticking out; now I was oriented. Since it had already become quite light, there was not a second to lose. We ran across open ground, whistled by the first rifle bullets, toward our own lines. In the front French trench we encountered the patrol of Lieutenant von Kienitz. When we heard the call "Lüttje Lage!" we knew that the worst was behind us. Unfortunately, I fell from above onto seriously injured man whom they had lying between them. Kienitz hastily told me that he had driven off a Frenchman that was working on entrenchments in the first trench with hand grenades and that he was subsequently killed by our artillery fire.

After a long wait, two of my men appeared, Sergeant Dujesiefken and Fusilier Haller, who brought me at least a small consolation prize. While wandering around alone, he had stumbled into a small trench and discovered three abandoned machine guns, one of which he had unscrewed from its frame and taken with him. As the sunlight became brighter and brighter, we hurried across no man's land to our front line.

Of the fourteen men who had gone out with me, only four returned, and the Kienitz patrol also suffered heavy losses. My discouragement was somewhat brightened by the words of the honest Oldenburger Dujesiefken, who, when I had my hand bandaged in the tunnel, reported the events to his comrades at the entrance and concluded with the sentence: "But now I have much respect for Lieutenant Jünger; boy, how he dashed over those barricades!"

We then marched through the forest to the regimental command post. Colonel von Oppen greeted us and had coffee poured for us. He was very saddened by our failure, but expressed all his appreciation for what we had accomplished. Then I was packed into a car and driven to the division, which wanted an exact report. Only a few hours ago I had been storming through shot-up trenches in a wild hand grenade fight, and now I was fully enjoying the pleasure of leaning back and cruising along the country road.

The general staff officer received me in his office and tried in vain to prove to me that I had been responsible for the loss of my men by hasty action. I thought, "You can make up any story you want here, twenty kilometers behind the front trench," and indicated to him that I had neither a green table in the enemy line, nor the maps on it. Besides, I had only had the honor of fighting. The plan, in which I found many things objectionable, had been put into my hand ready-made. I had previously asked to move the point of attack to the prominent line of the road or at least to shoot up colored flares from my own trench to show the way for the men who were lost. I had been told that this would attract enemy fire. Hell, what do I care about enemy fire? I'm used to it. But I am not an owl that finds its way in the dark!

The division commander greeted me very kindly and soon dispelled my bad mood. At lunch I sat next to him in a worn field coat with a bandaged hand and tried to put our actions of the morning in the right light after the words: "Only the louts are modest!"

The next day, Colonel von Oppen revisited the patrol, distributed Iron Crosses and gave each participant a fortnight's leave. In the afternoon, the fallen, whose repatriation had been successful, were buried in the military cemetery of Thiaucourt. Among the graves of this war there also rested combatants of 1870/71. One of these old graves was decorated by a mossy stone with the simple inscription:

"Far from the eye, eternally near to the heart!"

On a large stone tablet was chiseled:

"Heroic deeds, heroic graves line up anew with the old ones;
Proclaiming how the empire arose,
Proclaiming how the empire survived."

In the evening I read in the French army report: "A German enterprise near Regniéville failed; prisoners were taken." That the prisoners were taken only because our men had lost their way in the search for the uprooted enemy was not included. Had the French defended their trenches, as brave soldiers are wont to do, things might have turned out differently.

A few months later, I received a letter from one of the missing, Fusilier Meyer, who had lost a leg in a hand grenade fight there; he and three comrades had been involved in a fight after wandering around lost for a long time, badly wounded, and had been captured after the others had fallen, including the good sergeant Kloppmann.

I had many adventures during the war, but none of them was more frightening. I still get into an anxious mood when I think of our odyssey through the unknown trenches illuminated by the cold early morning light.

A few days later Lieutenants Domeyer and Zürn, along with several escorts, jumped into the first French line after some shrapnel shots. Domeyer came upon a French soldier with a powerful full beard, who returned his request: "Rendez-vous!" with a grim "Ah non!" and pounced on him. In the course of a fierce wrestling match, Domeyer shot him through the neck with his pistol and, like me, had to return without a prisoner. The only difference was that in my enterprise artillery ammunition was wasted that would have been enough for an entire battle in 1870.

XIV

Return to Flanders

O N the same day that I returned from my fortnight's leave, we were relieved by the 5th Bavarian Reserve Infantry Regiment and housed initially in the nearby village of Labry, one of the typical dirt nests of that region. What struck me most in these Lorraine villages was the futile search for a secluded locality. A bathtub seemed to be one of the unknown things. In this respect, I had some strange experiences in France. Even in the most magnificent castles, one had to ignore certain shady aspects with a discreet smile. As much as I appreciate the Frenchman, I consider this side of his nature to be a significant one.

> "What's the harm if the cesspool in the back runs and stinks,
> As long as the door knob in front shines and blinks."

On October 17, 1917, we were loaded onto a train and after a day and a half we set foot again on the soil of Flanders, which we had left only two months before. We spent the night in the small town of Iseghem and the next morning marched to Roulers or, as it is called in Flemish, Roselaire. The town was in the first stages of destruction. Goods were still being hawked in the stores, but the population was already squatting in the cellars, and the bonds of civic life had been broken by the frequent shelling. A shop window with ladies' hats opposite my quarters made a strangely out-of-place impression on me in the tumult of war. At night, looters tried to break into the abandoned shops and apartments.

In my quarters, located in Oststraat, I was the only occupant of the rooms above ground. The house belonged to a draper who had fled at the beginning of the war, leaving an old landlady and her daughter to guard it. The two of them were caring for a little girl whom they had found wandering the streets during our advance, abandoned by her parents. They did not even know the child's age or name. They had a fabulous fear of bombs and, almost on their knees, implored me not to turn on any lights upstairs so as not to attract the evil fliers. While I was standing next to Lieutenant Reinhardt at the window, watching an Englishman flying closely over the roofs in the light of the searchlights, a giant shell hit near the house and the air pressure blew out the window panes, sending glass shards all around our ears.

I was designated scout officer for the upcoming action and assigned to the regimental staff. In order to get my bearings, I went to the command post of the 10th Bavarian Reserve Regiment, which we were to relieve, even before our deployment. I found the commander to be a very friendly gentleman, although, at first he grumbled a bit when he saw my cap with the famous "red band," which was against the rules — red ribbons tend to attract bullets to the head. At that time, I had long since ceased to attach importance to an assorted field suit.

Two orderlies led me to the so-called reporting head, which was supposed to provide a very good overview. We had hardly left the command post when a shell hit right next to us. "Here I am, the much-loved son of Chaos!" Meanwhile, my guides very skillfully dodged the impact, which turned into an incessant drum roll around noon, in the terrain masked by numerous small poplar groves.

At the entrance of a secluded homestead, which showed the traces of fresh impacts, we saw a dead man lying on his stomach. "He's been wiped out!" uttered the plain Bavarian. "This is a bad spot," said the other with a sniffing look around and quickly moved on. The reporting head laid beyond the heavily shelled Paschendale-Westroosebeke road and proved to be a reporting collection point similar to the one I had run at Fresnoy. It was next to a house that had been shelled into a pile of rubble and had so little cover that the first cruder hit would destroy it completely. I was briefed on the enemy, the position, and the approach by three officers who were living a sociable cave existence there and were very pleased to be relieved so soon, and then returned to Roulers via Roodkruis-Oostnieukerke, where I reported to the colonel.

On the way through the streets of the city I read with pleasure the cozy names of the numerous small taverns, which so rightly expressed the Flemish sedateness. Who would not be attracted by a business sign with the title "De Zalm" (The Salmom), "De Reeper" (The Heron), "De Nieuwe Trompette" (The New Trumpet), "De drie Koningen" (The Three Kings) or "Den Olifant" (The Elephant)? Doesn't that sound like Teniers and De Coster? Already the welcome in the strong un-welted language with the familiar "Du" puts you in a comfortable mood. God grant that this splendid country may be resurrected in its old essence from the terrible wounds of this war.

In the evening, the city was bombarded again. I went down into the cellar, where the women had taken refuge, huddled together, shivering in a corner, and flicked on my flashlight to calm the little girl, who was screaming in terror in the dark because an explosion had put out the light. Here again it was evident how firmly man is fused to his homeland. Despite the tremendous fear these women had of danger, they clung tightly to the clod of earth that, at any moment, could become a grave.

On the morning of October 22nd, I set out with my scouting party of four men for Kalve, where the regimental staff was to be relieved. A tremendous fire was raging at the front, the flashes of which gave the early morning fog the appearance of a seething, blood-red steam. At the entrance to Oostnieukerke, a house next to us, hit by a heavy shell, collapsed with a crash. Stone debris rolled across the road. We tried to avoid the place, but had to pass through, since we did not know the direction to Roodkruis-Kalve. In passing, I asked a Bavarian sergeant, who was standing in the entrance to a cellar, for directions. Instead of answering, he buried his hands in his pockets and shrugged his shoulders. Since I had no time to lose due to the constantly falling shells, I jumped towards this product of a failed military training and forced information through the pistol held under his nose. If the man has not fallen or deserted in the meantime, he will certainly have enriched the Spartacus group with a worthy member.

At Roodkruis, a small homestead on a fork in the road, things became precarious. Bullets whizzed across the shelled road, infantry squads snaked through the terrain on either side, and countless wounded dragged themselves back from the front. One young artilleryman we encountered had a long, jagged piece of shrapnel sticking out of his shoulder. We turned right off the road to the regimental command post, which was surrounded by a strong wreath of fire. Nearby, two telephonists were laying line across a cabbage field. Immediately next to one of them a shell struck; we saw him fall and thought he was done for. However, he rose again immediately and continued to pull his wire with commendable cold-bloodedness. Since the command post consisted of only a tiny concrete block, with barely enough room for the commander with his adjutant and orderly officer, I had to seek shelter nearby. I moved into a light wooden barracks with the intelligence, gas protection, and mortar launcher officers, which was not exactly the ideal bomb-proof shelter.

In the afternoon, I went into position, since the report had come in that the enemy had attacked our 5th Company in the morning. My way led me over the signal head to the "North Yard," a farmstead shot up beyond recognition, under the ruins of which the commander of the riot battalion was living. From there, a path, though only hinted at, led to the combat troop's commander. Due to the heavy rains of the last few days, the conspicuous crater field had turned into a sea of mud, which, especially in the Paddebach valley, was life-threatening in depth. On my wanderings I passed many a lonely or forgotten dead bodies; often only the head or a hand was seen protruding above the dirty mirror of the craters. Thousands slumber in this way, without a cross erected by a friend to adorn the unknown gravesite.

After the extremely strenuous crossing of the Paddebach, made possible only by a few felled poplars lying across it, I discovered the leader of the 5th Company, Lieutenant Heins, in a giant crater, surrounded by a small, faithful squad. The crater was situated on a slope and, since it was not completely flooded, could be considered habitable by unassuming front-line soldiers. Heins told me that in the morning a line of English riflemen had appeared and then disappeared as soon as the shelling began. They in turn had shot some stray 164s that had run away on their approach. Otherwise everything was in order; I therefore returned to the command post, where I reported to the colonel.

The next day our lunch was rudely interrupted by some shells that hit in front of our door, their fountains of dirt drumming in a slow whirl on our tarred cardboard roof. Everyone rushed out of the door; I fled to a nearby homestead and went inside because of the rain. In the evening the process was repeated, only this time I stopped in front of the house, since weather was nice and sunny. The next shell hit the center of the house. That's how chance plays in war. More than elsewhere, it is true here: "Small causes, big effects." Seconds and millimeters decide.

At 8 o'clock in the morning on the 25th, we were driven out of the barracks due to a heavy impact — the one opposite us received a direct hit by the second shot. Inspired by the experiences of the previous day, I chose a lonely, trustworthy shell hole in the large coal field behind the regimental command post, from which I never left, except after a sufficiently long interval of safety. During this day I received the news, which was very personal to me, of the death of Lieutenant Brecht, who as a scout officer of the division. He had met his heroic death in the crater field to the right of the North Yard. I had always admired Brecht as a role model — he was living proof of the saying: "Fortes fortuna adiuvat" (Fortune favors the brave). He was one of the few who, as a result of their tireless bravado, were surrounded by a romantic nimbus even in this most prosaic of wars.

The morning hours of the 26th passed under a barrage of extraordinary ferocity. Our artillery also redoubled its fury in response to the barrage signals rising from the front. Every little patch of wood and every hedge was peppered with guns, behind which half-deaf artillerymen did their duty.

Since the returning wounded gave unclear and exaggerated information about an English attack, I was sent forward with my four men at 11 o'clock to reconnoiter more precisely. Our way led through sharp fire. We encountered numerous wounded, among them Lieutenant Spitz, leader of the 12th Company, who was shot in the chin. When we arrived in front of the K. T. K. hut we came into well-directed machine-gun fire, proof that the enemy must have broken through our lines. This suspicion was confirmed to me by Major Dietlein, leader of the 3rd Battalion. I found this old gentleman crawling on his belly out of the entrance of his concrete block, three-quarters of which was submerged in water, eagerly fishing for something that he had dropped in the mud. If only every German would have made such an effort regardless of age and health.

The enemy had penetrated the front line and taken over a ridge from which they could easily take aim at the Paddebach valley, where the K. T. K. was established. After I had marked this change of position on my map with a few blue-pencil strokes, I set out with my men on a new endurance run through the mud. While sprinting, we jumped over the area we had seen until we were behind the next bump in the road, and from there we slowed our pace before reaching the North Yard. Shells slammed into the swamp to the right and left of us, hurling up massive fountains of mud surrounded by countless smaller ones. The North Yard was under nerve-shattering brisance fire and had to be overcome by leaps and bounds. A shrapnel threw its charge of bullets between us with multiple claps. One of my companions was hit on the rear rim of his steel helmet and thrown to the ground. After lying stunned for a while, he picked himself up and kept running. The area around the North Yard was covered with a lot of terribly mangled corpses. After we had happily crossed the heavily shelled ground behind the Paschendale-Westroosebeke road, I was able to report to the regimental commander.

The next morning I was sent forward as early as 6 o'clock with the order to determine whether and where the regiment would have a connection. On the way I met Sergeant-Lieutenant Ferchland, who had to deliver the order to the 8th Company to advance on Goudberg and, if there should be one, to fill the gap between us and the left neighboring regiment. In order to carry out my order as quickly as possible, I could do no better than to join up. After a long search we found the leader of the 8th Company, Lieutenant Tebbe, who was a friend of mine, in an inhospitable part of the crater country near the Meldekopf. He was not very pleased about the order to carry out such a conspicuous movement in broad daylight. We lit a cigar during our meager conversation, depressed by the unspeakable sobriety of the morning-lit crater field, and waited for the company to gather. After only a few steps we received well-directed infantry fire from the opposite heights and had to advance one by one from crater to crater. On crossing the next slope, the fire became so concentrated that Tebbe gave orders to occupy a whole line of those ditches and wait there until night for the protection of darkness. Smoking a cigar, he walked the entire section with great cold-bloodedness to divide his groups.

I decided to proceed further to determine the size of the gap and rested for a moment in Tebbe's crater. Already the enemy artillery began to pour in on the strip of ground as punishment for the bold action of the company. A shell hit the edge of our place of refuge, splashing my eyes and map with wet clay, warning me to leave. I said goodbye to Tebbe and wished him good luck for the next few hours. As I was walking away he yelled, "Dear God, let it be night, tomorrow morning will come alone!"

We walked cautiously through the Paddebach valley, hiding behind the masses of fallen poplars and using their trunks as bridges. From time to time, one of us would disappear up to his hips in the mud and would have infallibly drowned if it hadn't been for the rifle butts of his comrades. I chose as my marching point a group of men surrounding a concrete block. In front of us, a stretcher towed by four medics was moving in the same direction. Puzzled by the observation that a wounded man was being dragged forward, I looked through the glass and caught sight of a row of khaki figures wearing flat steel helmets. At that moment, the first shots rang out. Since taking cover was impossible, we ran back while the bullets splattered into the mud all around us. The rush through the mud was insanely exhausting; but when we stood for a while as a target for the English, completely fatigued, a volley of brisance grenades gave us our old freshness back. It had, after all, the advantage of removing us from enemy view by the smoke it created. The most unpleasant thing about this run was the consciousness of being infallibly turned into a bog body by the slightest wound. I deduced from the trickles of blood from individual craters that many had already disappeared here.

Exhausted to death, we reached the regimental command post, where I handed in my sketches and reported on the situation.

On October 28th we were again relieved by the 10th Bavarian Reserve Regiment and, ready for constant intervention, were placed in the villages behind the front. The staff moved to Most.

In the evening we were again sitting in the room of an abandoned tavern, drinking wine and celebrating the promotion and engagement of Lieutenant Zürn, who had just returned from leave. As punishment for this carelessness, we were awakened the following morning by a giant drum fire, which, despite the distance, still blew out my window panes. Immediately after that the alarm was sounded. The rumor was that the enemy had entered at the still existing gap to the left of the regimental position. I spent the day waiting for orders at the observation post of the A. O. K., whose surroundings were under weak scattered fire. A light shell went through the window of a hut, from which three wounded artillerymen tumbled out, covered from head to toe in brick dust. Three others laid as corpses under the rubble.

The following morning I received the following order from the Bavarian commander: "As a result of the enemy's renewed advance, the position of the neighboring regiment on the left has been pushed back even more and the gap between the two regiments has widened considerably. As there was danger of the regiment's position being bypassed from the left, the 1st Battalion of the 73rd Fusilier Regiment counterattacked yesterday evening, but was apparently mauled by the barrage and did not reach the enemy. This morning the 2nd Battalion was sent forward towards the gap. Message has not yet arrived. It is necessary to survey the position of the 1st and 2nd Battalion to be reconnoitered."

I set off and met Captain von Brixen, commander of the 2nd Battalion, at the Nordhof, who already had the formation sketch in his pocket. I copied the drawing and had actually completed my mission, but went to the concrete block of the K. T. K. to get a personal overview. On the way there was a lot of fresh corpses lying on the ground, whose pale faces stared out of water-filled craters or were already so covered with mud that one could hardly recognize their human form. Unfortunately, the blue Gibraltar ribbon shone from the sleeves of most of them. The combat troop commander was the Bavarian Captain Rademeyer. This extremely energetic officer told me in detail what Captain von Brixen had already hastily told me. Our 2nd Battalion had suffered great losses, among others the battalion adjutant and the leader of the good 7th Company had fallen. The fate of the adjutant, Lieutenant Lemière, was particularly tragic, since his brother, leader of the 8th Company, had met his death at Fresnoy only that April. The two brothers were Liechtenstein nationals, yet joined the army out of enthusiasm for the German cause. It is not good to send two sons to war in the same regiment. We had four pairs of brothers in the officer corps. Of these eight young people, five fell, and two, including my brother, were brought home seriously injured. I am the only one who came out practically in one piece. This small example illustrates the losses of the Fusilier Regiment.

The captain pointed to a concrete block two hundred meters in front of ours, which was heroically defended yesterday. Shortly after the attack, the commander of the small fort, a sergeant, saw an Englishman carrying off three German prisoners. He shot the Englishman down and reinforced his garrison with the three men. When they ran out of ammunition, they put the wounded Englishman in front of the door as a peaceful figurehead. They were able to retreat unnoticed after nightfall.

Another concrete blockhouse commanded by a lieutenant was ordered to surrender by an English officer; instead of a reply, the German lieutenant jumped out, grabbed the Englishman and pulled him inside, right in front of his stunned English comrades.

On that day, for the only time in the war, I saw small squads of stretcher bearers with raised Red Cross flags moving openly in the zone of infantry fire without a shot being fired at them. Such images appeared to the front-line warrior in this underground war only when the hardship had risen to a point that was unbearable. Nevertheless, I later learned that concealed English gunners had shot down some of our stretcher bearers.

Many readers will consider this act to be the height of depravity, and yet I can explain that weak natures succumb to the atavistic urge to destroy, which seizes the trench warrior accustomed to solitude when men appear on the other side. I have felt it myself only too often.

My way back was made more difficult by an unpleasant irritant gas emitted from English shells, giving off the stench of rotten apples, which had settled in the ground and made my eyes water profusely. Immediately afterwards I was to experience an even more painful reason for shedding tears. After I had reported to the command post, I came across the stretchers of two officers who had been seriously wounded and who were friends of mine. One of them was Lieutenant Zürn, whom we had just celebrated in a merry circle two evenings before. Now he was laying on a door which had been torn off its hinges, half undressed, with that waxy-yellow complexion which is a sure omen of death, and looked at me with glassy eyes as I approached to squeeze his hand. The other, Lieutenant Haverkamp, had his arm and leg bones so shattered by shell fragments that amputation was very likely. He was laying on a stretcher, pale as a corpse, his features petrified with fatalism, smoking a cigarette.

In these days we had appalling losses of young officers. Every time I hear the derogatory judgment of the masses today about the war lieutenant, I have to think of these men who embodied the old Prussian spirit of duty and honor, the spirit of Kolin, out in the mud and blood, upright to the bitter end.

On November 3rd, we were loaded at Gits station, which we knew well from our first days in Flanders. We saw the two Flemish women again, but they had lost their good humor. They too seemed to have come back from long days of battle.

We stayed for some time in Tourcoing, a respectable sister city of Lille. For the first and last time in the war, every man of the 7th Company slept a feather bed. I occupied a splendidly furnished room in the house of an industrial baron in the Rue de Lille. With unspeakable pleasure I enjoyed the first evening in an armchair in front of the fire of the inevitable marble fireplace.

The few days were used by all to rejoice in the hard-won existence. One could hardly believe that one had escaped death. One felt the compulsion to make the most of life, to enjoy it in all its forms.

XV

The Battle of Cambrai

THE beautiful days of Tourcoing were soon over. We stayed for a short time at Villers-au-tertre, where we were replenished with new troops, and on November 15, 1917, we left for Lécluse, the staging area of the respective rest battalion of the position assigned to us. Lécluse was a larger Artois village surrounded by lakes. The extensive reed beds harbored ducks and water fowl, and the waters were teeming with fish. Although fishing was strictly forbidden, mysterious sounds were often heard on the water at night. One day the local command sent me some identification cards belonging to men from my company who had been caught fishing with hand grenades. However, I did not mention it to my men, since the good mood of the crew was much more important to me than the protection of the French hunt or the midday meals of the local commander. Since then, almost every evening a giant pike was placed on my table by an unknown hand. The next day for lunch I had some "Pike à la Lohengrin" prepared for my two company officers.

On the 19th, together with my platoon leaders, I visited the position we were to occupy in the next few days. It was located in front of the village of Vis-en-Artois. However, we did not get into the trenches as quickly as we had thought, since almost every night alarms were sounded and we were made available alternately in the Wotan position, the artillery barrage, or the village of Dury, because of a suspected English attack. It was clear to experienced warriors that this would not turn out well for us.

In fact, on November 29th, we learned from our battalion commander, Captain von Brixen, that we were to participate in a large-scale counterattack on the positional arc that the tank battle of

Cambrai had pushed into our front. Although we were glad to be able to exchange the role of the anvil with that of the hammer at last, we had misgivings, since most of our men were still quite worn out from Flanders. Nevertheless, I had confidence in the spirit of my company and its iron backbone, the experienced platoon leaders and excellent noncommissioned officers.

On the night between November 30th and December 1st, we were loaded into trucks. In the process, my company suffered its first casualties when one of the men accidentally dropped a hand grenade, which mysteriously exploded, severely wounding him along with a comrade. Another man tried to feign madness in order to escape the battle. I didn't know whether to laugh or get angry. At last he regained his senses with a strong jab to the ribs from a non-commissioned officer and we were finally able to board. We drove, cramped together, to the edge of Baralle, where we waited in a ditch for hours for our orders. I laid down in a meadow despite the cold and slept until dawn. We learned with some disappointment that 225th Regiment, to which we were attached, had renounced our participation in the storm. Meanwhile, we were to wait in reserve in the castle park of Baralle.

At 9 a.m., our artillery engaged in massive bursts of fire, which condensed into a barrage from 11:45 to 11:50. The Bourlon Forest disappeared under clouds of yellow-green gas, which, because of its strong fortifications, was not attacked head-on but left alone. At 11:50, through the lens of our scope, we saw lines of riflemen diving out of the empty crater field, while in the rear batteries were bracing and rushing forward to change positions. A German airman shot down a tethered English balloon, whose observer parachuted out.

After enjoying this battle panorama, which we had viewed from the heights of the castle park, we finished off a cooking pot full of noodles, laid down on the ground for an afternoon nap despite the cold, and at 3 o'clock received orders to advance to the regimental command post, which was hidden in the sluice chamber of a dried-up canal basin. We covered this distance, platoon by platoon, under a weak scattering fire. From there the 7th and 8th Companies were sent forward to the reserves commander to relieve two companies of the

225th Regiment. The five hundred yards that had to be covered in the bed of the canal were under dense fire. We ran to the objective without casualties, bunched together in a tight group. Numerous dead revealed that more than one company had already paid a bloody toll here. Reserves laid pressed close to the embankments and were busy digging cover holes in the bricked walls with feverish haste. Since all the places were occupied and the site was drawing fire as a terrain marker, I led the company into a crater field to the right of it and left each individual to set up there. A piece of shrapnel rattled against my sidearm. Together with Lieutenant Tebbe, who had followed our example with his 8th Company, I selected a suitable crater, which we covered with a canvas. We lit a candle, ate dinner, smoked our pipes and chatted while shivering. At 11 o'clock, I received orders to move into the former front line and report to the K. T. K., to whom the 7th Company was attached. I collected the men and led them forward. Only a few powerful shells hit, one of which shattered in front of us like a greeting from hell, filling the entire canal bed with dark smoke. The crew fell silent, as if they were being choked by an icy fist, and hastily followed my lead, stumbling over barbed wire and stone rubble. An indescribably unpleasant feeling creeps into the nerves when passing through an unknown position at night, even if the fire is not particularly strong. The warrior's eye and ear are put on alert by the strangest deceptions; he feels lonely between the looming walls of the trench like a child lost in a dark heath.

We finally found the narrow mouth of the first line into the canal and wound our way through crowded trenches to the battalion command post. I entered and found a bunch of officers and orderlies amid a Pantagruelian atmosphere. I learned that the attack had not accomplished much at this point and would be pushed further the next morning. The morale in the room left little to be optimistic about. Two battalion commanders began a long negotiation with their adjutants. From time to time, officers of the Special Weapons Corps threw a few chunks into the debate from the height of their bunkbeds, which were populated like a chicken coop. The cigar smoke became stifling. Attendants tried to cut sandwiches for their superiors in the throng. A wounded man rushing in raised a temporary alarm by reporting an enemy hand grenade attacked.

At last, I was able to write down my attack order. I was to clear up the Dragon Path with the company at 6 o'clock in the morning and, from there, push as far as I could to the Siegfried Line. The two battalions of the position regiment were to attack on our right at 7 o'clock. This time difference immediately aroused in me a very definite suspicion. I strongly objected to the fragmented attack and succeeded in getting us to line up at 7 o'clock as well. The next morning showed that this change was of great importance. The leader, experienced in war, can save his troops a lot of useless bloodshed in such cases.

A company that has been torn out of its association will not be pampered under foreign command. Since the location of the Dragon's Path was extremely mysterious to me, I asked for a map when I left, which I was told was indispensable. I said my piece and left.

After wandering around the position with the heavily packed men for a long time, a man spotted a sign with the half-smudged inscription "Dragon's Path" at a small trench branching off to the front, which was blocked by Spanish horsemen. As I went in, after only a few steps, I heard strange, murmuring voices. I was extremely surprised to find the enemy so close, almost in our own position, without any safety measures taken. I immediately ordered a group of men to block the trench.

Close to the Dragon's Path was a huge hole in the ground, apparently a tank trap, where I gathered the whole company to explain the combat mission and to divide the platoons for the attack. My speech was interrupted several times by small caliber shells. At one point a dud flew into the rear wall of the pit. I stood on top of the rim of the pit and saw a deep, solid bow of steel helmets, glistening in the moonlight below me.

Worried about a big unlucky hit, I sent the first and second platoons back to the position and stayed in the trench with the third. Crews of a detachment that had veered off in the Dragon's Path the previous noon made my men nervous by telling them that after fifty meters an English machine gun blocked the trench, creating an insurmountable obstacle. I then agreed with the platoon leaders to jump for cover on the right and left at the first resistance and attack concentrically with hand grenades. In the midst of the alien formation, it was especially important to uphold the regiment's honor at arms. I spent the endless hours huddled close to Lieutenant Hopf in a hole in the ground. At 6 o'clock, I rose and, in the peculiar mood that precedes every attack, made the final arrangements. One has a strange, sinking feeling in one's stomach, talks to the group leaders, tries to make jokes, walks back and forth as before a parade in front of the commanding general; in short, one seeks to occupy oneself as much as possible in order to escape the probing thoughts. A soldier offered me a cup of coffee heated over a flame, which conjured up warmth and confidence in the marrow of my bones.

At 7 o'clock sharp, we entered in the designated order in a long, single file line. We found the Dragon's Path unoccupied; a row of empty drums behind a barricade revealed that the machine gunner must have been withdrawn. Our spirit of attack was thus kindled. We entered a small sunken path after I had sealed off a well-made trench branching off to the right. The sunken path became shallower and shallower, and at last we found ourselves in an open field in the gray morning. We turned back and entered the trench on the right, which was stuffed full of war equipment and dead Englishmen. It was the Siegfried position. Suddenly the leader of the assault groups, Lieutenant Hoppenrath, snatched the rifle from one man's hand and fired. He had run into an English sentry who, after throwing a few hand grenades, took flight. We continued our march until we were met with renewed resistance. Hand grenades flew from both sides and exploded with multiple bangs. The storm troop technique kicked in. Flying projectiles traveled from man to man through the chain of hands; snipers nestled behind parapets targeted enemy throwers, platoon leaders peered over cover to spot a counterattack in time, and light machine gun operators set up their weapons at firing positions.

After a short fight, excited voices rang out on the other side, and before we quite understood what was happening, the first Englishmen came toward us with their hands up. One by one they turned around the shoulder and unbuckled their belts, while our rifles and pistols were pointed menacingly at them. They were all young, strapping guys in new uniforms. I let them pass with the command, "Hands down!" and assigned a group of men to take them back to our position. Most of them showed by their confident smiles that they did not expect anything inhuman from us. Others tried to make us merciful by holding out packs of cigarettes and chocolate bars. With the heightened joy of a hunter, I saw that we had made an enormous catch; the procession was never-ending. We had already counted one hundred and fifty men, and new ones were still appearing with arms raised. I stopped an English officer and asked him about the layout and the occupation of their position. He answered very politely, but he interfered with the good impression he made on me by standing at attention. He then escorted me to the leader of the company, a wounded captain, who was in a nearby shelter. I found a young man of about twenty six with a fine-cut face leaning against the shelter frame with a shot through his calf. When I introduced myself, he raised his hand, from which flashed a gold chain, to his cap, gave his name, and handed me his pistol. His first words showed that I had a real man before me. "We were completely surrounded." I urged him to explain to his adversary why his company had surrendered so quickly. We conversed in French about various things. He told me that a number of wounded Germans, bandaged and fed by his men, were lying in a nearby dugout. When I inquired how strongly the Siegfried position was occupied further back, he refused to give me any information. After I had promised to have him and the other wounded brought to the back, we said goodbye with a handshake.

In front of the entrance to the dugout my men reported that we had taken two hundred prisoners. A fine achievement for a company of eighty men. After I had issued sentry postings, we looked around the captured trench, which was overflowing with weapons and equipment. On the post stands were machine guns, mortars, hand and rifle grenades, canteens, fur vests, rubber coats, canvas tents, cans of meat, jam, tea, coffee, cocoa and tobacco, cognac bottles, tools of the trade, pistols, flare guns, linen, gloves, in short everything you could think of. I took a little break to give my men time to rest and examine the good stuff a little closer. I, too, could not resist the temptation to have my lad put together a little breakfast in the entrance of the shelter and light a pipe of the long-desired navy cut tobacco while I scribbled my report to the combat troop commander. Being a cautious man, I sent a duplicate to our battalion commander.

After half an hour we re-entered in a state of euphoria (I will not deny that the English cognac bottles may have contributed a little) and stalked along the Siegfried position from one side to the other.

We received fire from a blockhouse built into the trench. To get our bearings on the situation, we climbed to the next post. While we were exchanging a few bullets with the occupants, one man was knocked to the ground as if by an invisible fist. A bullet had pierced the top of his steel helmet and tore a long groove in the top of his skull. His brain rose and fell back into the wound with each pulse of blood, yet he was still able to walk to the back alone.

I called for volunteers to break the resistance by attacking across open ground. The men looked at each other hesitantly; only a clumsy Pole, whom I had always thought to be stupid, climbed out of the trench and trudged heavily toward the blockhouse. Now Ensign Neupert and his platoon also jumped out, while we proceeded simultaneously in the trench. The English fired a few shots and fled, leaving the blockhouse to us. One of the ensign's men had collapsed dead in the middle of the run-up and was lying with his face on the ground a few steps from the target.

As we proceeded, we encountered fierce opposition from invisible hand grenade throwers and, in the course of a prolonged slaughter, were pushed back to the blockhouse. There we barricaded ourselves. Both we and the English left a number of corpses in the embattled trench section. Unfortunately, among them was Sergeant Mevius, whom I had learned to appreciate as a foolhardy fighter on the night of Regniéville. He was lying with his face in a large pool of blood. When I turned him over, I saw from a large hole in his forehead that no more help was needed.

After the enemy had also retreated somewhat, a stubborn firefight began, during which a Lewis rifle, posted fifty meters in front of us, forced our heads down. A light machine gunner of ours took up the duel. For half a minute the two murder weapons, splattered with bullets, rattled away at each other. Then our gunner, Fusilier Motullo, collapsed with a shot to the head. Although his brains were running down his face to his chin, he was still in his right mind when we carried him into the next shelter. Gradually things quieted down a bit, as the English were also working on a barricade. At 12 o'clock, Captain von Brixen, Lieutenant Tebbe and Lieutenant Vogt appeared and congratulated me on the success of the company. We sat down in the blockhouse, ate breakfast from the English supplies and discussed the situation. In the meantime, I was shouting and negotiating with about twenty five Englishmen whose heads emerged from the trench a hundred meters in front of us and who apparently wanted to surrender. As soon as I rose above cover, however, I was fired upon from further back.

Suddenly there was movement at the barricade. Hand grenades flew. Rifles cracked, machine guns rattled. "They are coming! They're coming!" We jumped behind the sandbags and fired. One of my men, Fusilier Kimpenhaus, jumped on top of the barricade in the heat of battle and fired into the trench until two heavy shots to the arm swept him down. I remembered this hero of the moment and had the pleasure of congratulating him on his Iron Cross fourteen days later.

No sooner had we returned from this little interlude to our breakfast when a new pandemonium broke out. One of those strange incidents occurred, in which the history of war, large and small, is so rich. The shouting came from a deputy officer of the neighboring regiment on the left, who wanted to establish contact with us and was animated by a tremendous lust for brawling. Alcohol ingestion seemed to have inflamed his innate bravado to a frenzied madness. "Where's the Tommy? Let's get the dogs! Come on, who's coming?" In his fury, he tore down our beautiful barricade and rushed forward, clearing his path with cracking hand grenades. In front of him, his orderly slid through the trench and finished off those who had escaped the explosives with rifle shots.

Courageous, foolhardy use of one's own person always has an inspiring effect. We, too, were seized by daredevilry and, gathering up a few hand grenades, hurried to take part in the improvised assault. Soon I found myself next to the officer's deputy, and the other

THE BATTLE OF CAMBRAI

officers, followed by men from my company, did not take long either. Even the battalion commander, Captain von Brixen, was among the foremost with a rifle in his hand and struck down several enemy throwers over our heads.

The English fought back valiantly. There was a struggle for every shoulder defense. The black balls of the Mill hand grenades crossed in the air with our stick grenades. Behind every taken shoulder gun we found corpses or bodies that were still twitching. Men were killing each other without seeing each other. We also had casualties. Next to the orderly, a piece of steel fell to the ground and the man could not avoid it; he collapsed while his blood seeped from many wounds onto the clay.

We jumped over his body and continued forward. Thunder crackled on our way. Behind rifle and machine gun, hundreds of eyes lurked for a target in the dead terrain. We were already far ahead of our own lines. Bullets whistled around our steel helmets from all sides or shattered with a hard thud on the edge of the trench.

A trench branching off to the right was cleared out by men of the 225th Regiment advancing in our wake. Englishmen caught in a bind tried to escape across an open field and were shot down as if in a drive hunt.

Then came the climax; the breathless enemy, whom we had kept hard on our heels, made an effort to escape through a connecting trench that turned to the right. I jumped on a post and saw that this trench ran parallel to ours for a distance of twenty meters. So the enemy had to pass us once more. From our elevated position we could see directly on the steel helmets of the Englishmen who were stumbling with haste and excitement. I hurled a hand grenade at the feet of the foremost ones, so that they stopped in stupor, and those following them were wedged in. Now there was an indescribable destruction; hand grenades flew through the air like snowballs, enveloping everything in a whitish smoke. Two men continuously handed me ready projectiles. Lightning flashed between the huddled Englishmen, throwing up rags and steel helmets. Screams of rage and fear mingled. With fire in front of our eyes, we screamed and jumped on the edge of the trench.

In the middle of this frenzy I was thrown to the ground by a terrible blow. Sobered, I tore off my steel helmet and to my horror saw two large holes in it. The sergeant Mohrmann, who stood by me, calmed me down by assuring me that only a bleeding crack was visible on the back of my head. The bullet from a distant shooter had penetrated my steel helmet and grazed my head. Half stunned, I staggered back with my head bandaged to remove myself from this focal point of the battle. I had hardly passed the next shoulder guard when a man rushed up behind me and announced that Lieutenant Tebbe had just been shot in the head at the same place.

This terrible news did me in. I refused to believe the fact that a friend with whom I had shared joy, sorrow and danger for years, and who had shouted his last joke to me just a few minutes ago, should have met his end by a senseless piece of lead. Unfortunately, it was only too true.

At the same time, all the outstanding noncommissioned officers and a third of my company bled to death in this murderous little trench. Lieutenant Hopf also fell, an already elderly man, teacher by profession, ideal German schoolmaster in the best sense of the word. My two midshipmen and many others were wounded. Nevertheless, the 7th Company held the gloriously conquered position under the leadership of Lieutenant Hoppenrath, the last company officer, until relief came.

Modern combat also has its great moments. One so often hears the erroneous view that infantry combat has degenerated into an uninteresting mass slaughter. On the contrary, today more than ever the individual decides. Everyone knows this who has seen them in their realm, the princes of the trench with the hard, determined faces, daredevil, so sinewy, lithely leaping back and forth, with sharp, bloodthirsty eyes, heroes whom no report names. Trench warfare is the bloodiest, wildest, most brutal of all, but even it has had its men, men who were equal to their hour, unknown, daring fighters. Among all the nerve-racking moments of war, none is as powerful as the meeting of two shock troopers between the narrow mud walls of the trench. There is no turning back and no mercy. Blood rings from the shrill cry of recognition that wrings itself from the chest like nightmare pressure.

On the way back, I stopped next to the Captain von Brixen, who, with some men, was engaged in a firefight against a row of heads sticking out of a nearby parallel trench. I placed myself between him and another gunner and watched the bullet impacts.

Suddenly, another impact to my forehead threw me to the bottom of the trench, while my eyes were blinded by blood streaming down. The man next to me fell at the same time and began to wail. Head shot through steel helmet and temple. The captain feared that he had lost his 2nd Company commander that day, but on closer inspection found only two superficial lacerations at the hairline; probably caused by the shattering bullet or steel helmet fragments from the wounded man.

Weakened by the renewed loss of blood, I joined the captain, who went back to his command post. Overcoming the heavily shelled outskirts of Moeuvres at a run, we gained the shelter in the canal bed, where I received bandages and a tetanus shot.

In the afternoon I got into a truck and drove to Lécluse, where I reported to the enthusiastic Colonel von Oppen at dinner. After I had emptied a bottle of wine half asleep, but in an excellent mood, I took my leave and, after this tremendous day, with an after-work feeling, threw myself on the bed that my faithful, joyful Vinke had prepared for me.

The battalion moved into Lécluse the day after next. On December 4th, the division commander, Major General von Busse, gave an address to the participating battalions in which the merits of the 7th Company were particularly emphasized.

I could be justifiably proud of my men. Barely eighty men had captured a long trench section; captured a lot of machine guns, mortars and material, and taken two hundred prisoners. Unfortunately, we also had a casualty rate of fifty percent, including a particularly large number of batches. I had the pleasure of announcing a long series of promotions and awards. Deservedly, Lieutenant Hoppenrath, leader of the shock troops, Ensign Neupert, the blockhouse striker, and last but not least, the daring barricade defender Kimpenhaus, received the Iron Cross. I was given a fortnight's Christmas leave to let my fifth wound heal, during which time the Knight's Cross of the House Order of Hohenzollern with swords was sent to my home. In the course of the war, I acquired a peculiar view of orders, but I confess that I proudly pinned the gold-edged enamel cross to my chest. This cross, my steel helmet shot through and a silver cup with the inscription "To the victor of Moeuvres," given to me by the three other company leaders of the battalion, are my mementos of the battle of Cambrai.

XVI

At the Cojeul River

A FTER a few days of rest, we relieved the 10th Company in the front line on December 9, 1917. The position, as I have already reported, was in front of the village of Vis-en-Artois. My section of the company was bounded on the right by the Arras-Cambrai road and on the left by the marshy bed of the Cojeul river, across which we maintained communication with the adjoining company by night patrols. The enemy position was hidden from view by an elevation lying between the front trenches. Except for a few patrols tampering with our wire at night and the humming of a dynamo set up in the nearby Hubertus Farm, the enemy infantry was nowhere to be seen.

My shelter was dug into the steep wall of a quarry yawning behind the position, which was heavily shelled almost every day. Behind it, the iron scaffolding of a destroyed sugar factory loomed in grotesque desolation.

The quarry was an eerie place. Between the craters filled with spent war material were the crooked crosses of decayed graves. At night, one could not see one's hand in front of one's eyes and had to wait from the extinguishing of one flare for the other to rise, so as not to stray from the safe path of the running grates into the mud of the Cojeul ground.

When I was not working on the construction of the trench, I spent my days in the freezing cold dugout, reading a book and drumming my feet against the shelter's frame to keep them warm. The same purpose was served by the bottle hidden in a niche of the limestone, to which my orderlies and I were strongly attached.

If we had let the smoke of a fire rise from the quarry to the gloomy December sky, the place would have become completely uninhabitable, since the enemy seemed to think that the sugar factory was the seat of the command post and considered it accordingly. So it was not until the hour of dawn that life seeped back into our frozen limbs. The small stove was set on fire, spreading not only thick smoke but also a cozy warmth. Soon the cooking utensils of the food fetchers returning from Vis, who were already eagerly awaited, clattered on the shelter stairs. When the ceaseless succession of turnips, pearl barley and dried vegetables was interrupted by beans or noodles, the mood left nothing to be desired. Sometimes, sitting at my little table, I was delighted by the primitive conversation of the men who, wrapped in clouds of tobacco, squatted around the stove from which a cooking pot full of grog emitted strong smells. War and peace, battle and home, resting place and vacation were the topics discussed in a dry Lower Saxon style, eroticism also played a major role.

On December 17th, I started my vacation, from which I returned on January 2nd.

On January 19th, we were relieved at 4 a.m. and marched through dense snowstorm to Gouy, where we were to remain for some time to train for the tasks of the great offensive. Ludendorff's wonderfully clear training orders, which were distributed as far as the company commanders, held out the prospect of the attack for the next period.

We resumed the almost forgotten drills of infantry combat and movement warfare, and rifle and machine gun shooting was also eagerly practiced. Since all the villages behind the front were occupied up to the last attic, every embankment was used as a target stand, so that the bullets sometimes whirred across the terrain as if in a battle. A machine gunner of my company shot the commander of another regiment out of the saddle in the middle of a critique. Fortunately the wound was a minor one and our perpetration not clearly provable.

Several times I undertook practice attacks with live hand grenades on entangled trench systems with the company in order to evaluate our experience of the battle of Cambrai. Men were wounded in these exercises as well. Where wood is hewn, chips fall.

On January 24th, our Colonel von Oppen, revered by all, took leave to take over a brigade in the far southeast. The departure of this outstanding leader, who had become firmly attached to his troops during the long years of the war, was a painful loss to the entire regiment. In addition to a warm participation in the fortunes of his subordinates, he possessed the quality, not common among officers who had grown old in monotonous peacetime service, of being able to adapt with ease to the tremendous innovations of war. Such a man can accomplish immeasurable things in war. Unfortunately, his parting words: "See you in Hanover!" did not come true. Our dear colonel never saw his homeland or his proud regiment again. He rests in foreign soil, far from home, carried off by a treacherous cholera epidemic.

On February 6th, we moved back to Lécluse and, on the 22nd, were quartered for four days in the crater field on the left of the Dury-Hendecourt road to entrench in the front line at night. During the inspection of the position, which was opposite the heap of ruins of the former village of Bullecourt, it became clear to me that a part of the tremendous attack, of which there was expectant talk on the whole western front, was to take place there.

Construction was going on everywhere with feverish haste, tunnels were being driven and new roads were being laid out. The crater field was teeming with little signs standing in the middle of the terrain, on which incomprehensible numbers were written, apparently designating the places for batteries and command posts. The entire time our planes flew barricades to prevent enemy aircrafts from observing the camp. An interesting novelty at the front was that every noon at 12 o'clock sharp a black ball was lowered from the tethered balloons, which disappeared precisely ten minutes later. This was done to provide the troops with accurate time.

Toward the end of the month we marched back to our old quarters in Gouy. After several exercises in battalion and regimental formation, we twice practiced a breakthrough of the entire division at a large traced position. Afterwards the division commander made an address to his officers, during which it became clear to everyone that the storm was to break in the next few days. The brazen spirit of the attack, the spirit of the Prussian infantry, hovered over the masses who had gathered here on the northern French field at the spring awakening for the battle rehearsal.

If the goal set by the leadership was not achieved, it was not the fault of the officers and the men who, after 44 months of the heaviest fighting, threw themselves against the enemy with as much enthusiasm as ever in August 1914. Truly, the whole world had to stand in the breach to withstand such a storm. When, in the course of the years, the waves of hatred will have smoothed out, history will recognize that we have fought as no nation has ever fought before.

With pleasure I remember those evening hours when we sat together at the round table and talked with hot heads about the forthcoming fresh and cheerful movement of war. We exchanged our last thaler for wine in the enthusiasm. What did we need money for beyond the enemy lines or even in the better beyond?

> Who knows if the world won't
> Crumble into rubble tomorrow,
> As long as it holds today.
> Today is today!

The captain was able to remind us that the rear wanted to live after all; otherwise we would have smashed glasses, bottles and plates against the walls, on that last evening. The men were also in good shape. If you heard them talking in their dry Lower Saxon way about the upcoming "Hindenburg flat race," you knew they would tackle it as they always did, tenaciously, reliably, and without unnecessary shouting. How could one have been at the rear when they entered the fray, these silent sons of old, oak-fringed farms? Many gleaming ideals that hung over our goals were shattered by the war, but one thing remained forever: our unshakable loyalty.

On March 17th, after dark, we marched from the quarters we had already grown fond of to Brunemont. All the streets were crowded with restless marching columns, innumerable guns and endless trains. Nevertheless, precise order prevailed according to a mobilization plan worked out by general staff officers. Woe to the troops who did not scrupulously keep to the route and marching time; they were ruthlessly pushed into the ditch and had to wait for hours before they could squeeze into a gap. Once, however, we got into a scramble, during which the riding horse of Captain von Brixen impaled itself on an iron wagon drawbar and died.

XVII

The Great Battle

THE battalion was placed in the castle of Brunemont. We learned that we were to march forward during the night of March 19, 1918, to be staged near Cagnicourt in tunnels of the crater field, and that the great attack was to begin on the morning of the 21st. The regiment's mission was to push through between the villages of Ecoust-St. Mein and Noreuil, well known to us from 1915/16, and possibly reach Mory on the first day.

I sent Lieutenant Schmidt, whom we could not call anything else but "Schmidtchen" because of his kindness, ahead to secure the accommodation of the company.

At the appointed hour, the battalion marched off from Brunemont. Despite the pouring rain, the mood was good. I overlooked a drunk who was staggering between the limbs of my company, bawling. Right now any sharp words would only hurt. The training was over, now came the matter itself. One had to let every cog run.

From a road junction, where our guides were waiting for us, the companies marched forward independently. When we reached the height of the second line where we were to be placed, it turned out that our guides had lost their way. We began to wander in the dimly lit, muddy crater terrain, along with innumerable questioning, equally disoriented squads. In order not to completely exhaust my men, I had them stop and sent the guides out in different directions.

The groups put their rifles together and crowded into a huge crater, while I sat with Lieutenant Sprenger on the edge of a smaller one. For some time now, isolated impacts had been flaring up about a hundred meters in front of us. Another shell struck at a shorter distance; splinters slapped against the clay walls of the crater. One man cried out, claiming to have been hit in the foot. I shouted for the men to scatter into the surrounding holes while I examined the wounded man's muddy boot with my hands for a bullet hole. Then it whistled again high in the air; everyone had the same constricting feeling: it's coming here! Then there was a tremendous, deafening crash; the shell had struck right in the middle of us. . . . While half fainting, I straightened up. From the large crater an intense pink light emanated—our machine gun ammunition was on fire. It illuminated the smoldering smoke of the impact, in which black bodies twisted and the shadows of the survivors scattered from all sides. At the same time, there were multiple, horrible roars and screams for help.

I will not conceal the fact that at first, like everyone else, I jumped up after a moment of petrified horror and ran haphazardly into the night. Only in a small shell hole, into which I had fallen head first, the process became clear to me. No more hearing and seeing! Away, far away, crawl away! And yet immediately the other voice spoke up: "Gee, you're the company commander!" Exactly so. I do not say it to boast; I would rather say: to whom God gives an office, he also gives the spirit. I have often experienced in myself and others that the leader's sense of responsibility is drowned out by personal fear. One had a foothold, something to think about. So I forced myself back to the terrible place; on the way I came across Fusilier Haller, who had captured the machine gun during my November patrol, and took him with me.

The wounded were still uttering their terrible cries. Some came crawling toward me and whimpered, recognizing my voice: "Mr. Lieutenant! Mr. Lieutenant!" One of my dearest recruits, whose thigh had been crushed by a splinter, was clung to my legs. Cursing my inability to help, I patted him helplessly on the shoulder. One never forgets such moments.

I had to leave the unfortunates to the only surviving stretcher-bearer in order to lead the small group of faithful men that had gathered around me out of the endangered area. Half an hour ago, I was still at the head of a strong, excellent company, but now I was wandering through the trenches with a few people who were completely depressed. A milk-faced youth, who only a few days ago, mocked by his comrades, had carried over the heavy ammunition boxes from drill, still faithfully dragging this burden, which had saved him from the terrible scene, along our weary path. This observation broke me. I threw myself to the ground and erupted into convulsive sobs, while my men stood gloomily around me.

After several hours of unsuccessful dashing through trenches where mud and water stood a foot high, often threatened by impacting shells, we crawled, exhausted to death, into some ammunition niches built into the walls. My lad Vinke spread his blanket over me; nevertheless, due to the terrible nervous excitement, I could not close an eye and, smoking cigars, awaited the dawn.

The first light of day unveiled a quite incredible life in the crater field. Countless squads of infantry were still trying to reach their cover. Artillerymen hauled ammunition, mortarmen pulled their loads; telecommunicators and light signalists built lines. It was the purest fairground bustle a thousand meters in front of the enemy, who incomprehensibly seemed to notice nothing.

Fortunately, I came across the leader of the 2nd Machine Gun Company, Lieutenant Fallenstein, an old front-line officer, who was able to show me our quarters. His first words were, "Gee, what happened to you?" I led my men into a large dugout, which we must have passed a dozen times during the night, and in which I found Schmidtchen, who was not yet aware of our misfortune. I also found the guides. From that day on, whenever we took up a new position, I always chose the guides myself and with the greatest care. In war one learns thoroughly, but the price of learning is expensive.

After accommodating my companions, I set out for the previous night's scare site. The place looked gruesome. Around the burned impact site laid over twenty blackened corpses, almost all of them mangled beyond recognition. Some of the fallen had to be listed as missing later, since nothing of them could be found.

I found some soldiers of nearby units busy pulling out of the ghastly tangle the blood-stained belongings of the dead and searching them for loot. Disgusted, I chased the hyenas away and gave my orderly the task of collecting the wallets and valuables, as much as possible, in order to save them for the bereaved families. However, we had to leave them behind the following day during the storm.

To my delight, from a nearby tunnel, Lieutenant Sprenger was found with a crowd of people who had spent the night there. I had the squad leaders report and found that I still had sixty three men at my disposal. The night before I had left, in high spirits, with one hundred and fifty soldiers. I succeeded in determining over twenty dead and over sixty wounded, many of whom later succumbed to their injuries. The only small consolation was that it could have been even worse. For example, Fusilier Rust was standing so close to the impact that the straps of his ammunition boxes began to burn, yet he came through unscathed. Sergeant Peggau (who lost his life the following day) was standing between two men who were completely torn apart without even the slightest scratch.

We spent the day in a depressed mood, mostly sleeping. I frequently had to see the battalion commander, since there was always something to discuss about the attack. Otherwise I had a conversation with my two officers, lying on a cot, about the most trivial things in order to escape the torturing thoughts. The constant refrain was, "Thank God, the worst that can happen to us is death!" I made a short speech in an attempt to raise the morale of my men who were sitting silently on the stairs of the hut. But it seemed to have little effect. Clearly, I was not in the right frame of mind to encourage others.

At 10 o'clock in the evening, an orderly brought the order to march off to the front line. When an animal of the wild is dragged out of its den, or a sailor sees the saving plank sink beneath his feet, they may have feelings similar to ours when we had to part from the safe, warm dugout. However, not one of my men had the thought of staying behind unnoticed.

We rushed through the Felix Trench under sharp shrapnel fire and arrived in front without casualties. The battalion was assigned a very narrow section. All the dugouts were stuffed full of men in no time. The rest dug holes in the trench walls to have at least some protection during the artillery fire preceding the attack. After much toing and froing, everyone had found his place. Once again, Captain von Brixen gathered the company commanders for a briefing. After comparing our watches for the last time, we parted with a handshake.

I sat down next to my two officers on the staircase of a dugout to await the time of 5:05 a.m., when fire preparation was to begin. The mood had lightened somewhat as the rain had stopped and the starry night promised a dry morning. We spent the time talking and eating; there was heavy smoking, and the canteen made the rounds steadily. During the first hours of the morning the enemy artillery was so lively that we feared the Englishman had smelled a fuse.

Shortly before the start, the following radio announcement was made: "His Majesty the Kaiser and Hindenburg have gone to the scene of operations." It was greeted with applause.

The hand moved further and further; we counted the last minutes. Finally, the clock stood at five past five. The hurricane erupted. A furious thunder, which swallowed up even the heaviest launches in its mighty roll, made the earth tremble. The gigantic roar of annihilation from the countless guns behind us was so terrible that even the greatest of the battles we had survived seemed like child's play in comparison. What we had not dared to hope for happened: the enemy artillery remained silent; it was crushed with a single massive blow. We could not stand it any longer in the dugout. Standing on cover, we admired the wall of fire flaming above the English trenches, veiled behind billowing, blood-red clouds.

Our joy was disturbed by tears in the eyes and burning of the mucous membranes, caused by the fumes of our gas grenades driven back by the wind. The unpleasant effects of the blue cross gas forced many men to tear off their masks due to choking and coughing. I was very worried; however, I firmly trusted that our leadership could not possibly have made a calculation that would result in our undoing. Nevertheless, with the exertion of all my energy, I forced back the first cough so as not to further the irritation. After an hour we were able to take off our masks. It had become day. Behind us, the tremendous din grew continuously. In front of us, impenetrable to the eye, rose a wall of smoke, dust and gas. Men were running through the trench, shouting joyful cheers in each other's ears. Infantrymen and artillerymen, sappers and long-distance telephone operators,

Prussians and Bavarians, officers and enlisted men, all were overwhelmed, thrilled by this elemental expression of German strength, and eager to move in for the assault at 9:40. At 8:25 our heavy caliber shells intervened, standing in narrow gaps behind the front trench. We saw the huge two-ton shells fly through the air in a high arc and fall to the ground on the other side with volcano-like eruptions.

Even the laws of nature seemed to have lost their validity; the air shimmered like on hot summer days. The varying refraction exponent made solid objects dance back and forth. Black streaks of shadow darted through the clouds.

The last hour of preparation became more dangerous than the other four, during which we had moved quietly to cover. The enemy brought a heavy battery under fire, hurling shot after shot into our crowded full trench. To evade, I moved to the left and bumped into the adjutant, Lieutenant Heins, who asked me about Lieutenant Freiherr von Solemacher: "He must take over the battalion at once, Captain von Brixen has just fallen." Shocked by this terrible news, I went back and sat down in a deep hole in the ground. On my way down the short stretch of path I had already forgotten the fact. My brain had clung to reality only through the number 9:40. Meanwhile, it seemed like I was behaving very encouragingly, because all my men smiled at me approvingly.

In front of my hole in the ground, Sergeant Dujesiefken, my companion at Regniéville, stood and asked me to get into the trench, since the slightest impact could have buried me under masses of earth. An explosion tore the word from his mouth: with a torn leg he fell to the ground. I jumped over him and hurried to the right, where I crawled into a foxhole that was already occupied by two engineers. In a tight circle around us, the heavy projectiles continued their rampage. Suddenly black clods of earth were seen whirling out of a white cloud; the explosion was lost in the general roar. In fact, one could hear nothing at all. In the little trench to the left of us, three men of my company were torn to pieces. One of the last hits, a dud, killed poor Schmidtchen, who was still sitting on the stairs of the dugout.

I stood together with Sprenger, watch in hand, in front of my foxhole and awaited the great moment. The remnants of the company had gathered around us. We managed to cheer them up and distract them with offensive jokes that, unfortunately, cannot be reproduced here. Lieutenant Meyer, who peeked around the corner for a moment, later told me that he thought we had gone insane.

At 9:10 the officer patrols, which were to secure our formation, left the trench. Since the front lines were more than eight hundred meters apart, we had to line up, even before the artillery preparations were finished, and be ready in no man's land in such a way that we could jump into the first enemy line at exactly 9:40. Sprenger and I climbed over the parapet a few minutes later, followed by our men.

"Now let's show what the 7th Company is capable of!" "Now everything is up to us!" "Revenge for the 7th Company!" "Revenge for Captain von Brixen!" We drew our pistols and crossed our wire, through which the first wounded were already dragging themselves back.

I looked to the right and left. The divided line of two armies facing each other presented a bizarre image. In the craters in front of the enemy trench, which was being churned over and over again in the highest intensification of fire, the attack battalions were waiting in an unmistakably broad front, clumped together, company by company. At the sight of these huge, piled-up masses, the breakthrough seemed certain to me. But did we have the strength to break up the enemy reserves and tear them apart? I expected it with certainty. The final battle, the last attempt seemed to have come. The atmosphere was strange, charged with the utmost tension. Officers stood erect and shouted nervous jokes to each other. Often a heavy shell would fall short, throwing up a fountain as high as a church tower and showering us with earth without anyone even ducking his head. The thunder of battle had become so terrible that no one was in his right mind. The nerves were desensitized and could no longer feel fear.

Three minutes before the attack, my lad, the faithful Vinke, beckoned me with a canteen filled with cognac. His simple perspective recognized the need of the hour. I took a big swig, as if I were drinking water. Now the offensive cigar was still missing. Three times the air pressure extinguished my match.

Finally, the big moment had come. The drum of fire rolled over the first trenches. We stepped up.

In a mixture of emotions caused by blood thirst, anger and alcohol consumption, we walked towards the enemy lines. I was far ahead of the company, followed by my lad. My right hand clutched the pistol stock, my left a riding stick made of bamboo cane. I was seething with a fury now incomprehensible to me. The overpowering desire to kill quickened my steps. The rage brought bitter tears to my eyes.

The tremendous will to destruction that weighed over the battlefield was concentrated in my brain. This is how the men of the Renaissance may have been gripped by their passions, this is how a Cellini may have raced, werewolves howling through the night, thirsting for blood.

Without difficulty, we passed through a tattered tangle of wire and set off in a leap across the first trench. The storm troops danced like a series of ghosts through white, billowing mist.

Contrary to our expectations, machine gun fire rattled towards us from the second line. I jumped into a crater with my companions. A second later there was a terrible crash and I fell face-first to the ground. Vinke grabbed me by the lapels and turned me over on my back, "Are you wounded, Lieutenant?" There was nothing to be found. Though, one man had a hole in his upper arm and assured us, groaning, that a bullet had hit him in the back. We tore off his uniform and bandaged him up. The churned earth showed that shrapnel had hit the rim of the crater at the level of our faces. It was a miracle that we were still alive.

Meanwhile, the others had passed us by. We rushed after them, leaving the wounded man to his fate. In front, to our left, the mighty Ecoust-Croisilles railroad embankment, which we had to cross, emerged from the haze. Rifle and machine-gun fire pattered from built-in embrasures and dugout entrances.

Vinke had also disappeared. I followed along a trench, from whose embankment depressed dugouts yawned. Furious, I advanced forward over the black, torn-up ground, from which the stuffy gases of our grenades still hovered.

Then I caught sight of the first enemy. A figure crouched about three meters in front of me, apparently wounded, in the middle of the path. I saw him shudder at my appearance and stare at me with wide-open eyes as I walked toward him very slowly, my pistol extended. Gritting my teeth, I put the muzzle to the temple of the man paralyzed with fear; with a wail he reached into his pocket and held out a card before my eyes. It was the picture of him surrounded by a large family. . . . After seconds of inner struggle, I got myself together. I strode past the man without shooting him.

From above, men from my company jumped into the trench. I was burning hot. I tore off my coat and chucked it away. I remember that several times I shouted very energetically, "Now Lieutenant Jünger is taking off his coat!" and the fusiliers laughed at that, as if I had made the most delicious joke. Above, everyone ran around in the open, oblivious to the machine guns that were at most four hundred meters away. The instinct for annihilation also forced me into the sheaves of fire. I ran head-on into the fire-breathing railroad embankment. In some crater, I jumped on a pistol-packing figure in Manchester brown. It was Kius, who was in a similar mood and slipped me a handful of ammunition in greeting.

We must have been running crisscross through the craters for quite some time now, firing at various targets. In any case, I suddenly found myself at the foot of the railroad embankment and noticed that, close to me, a dugout entrance covered with burlap was being fired from. I shot through the cloth; a man next to me tore it away and threw a hand grenade into the opening, creating a shockwave and an escaping whitish cloud. The remedy was rough, but tried. The two of us ran along the embankment and worked the next hatches in a similar fashion. I raised my hand to notify our men, whose projectiles rang out around our ears at close range. They waved back joyfully. Then we climbed the embankment with a hundred others at the same time. For the first time in the war I saw large masses colliding. The English occupied two terraced trenches on the rear embankment. Bullets were exchanged within a few meters, hand grenades flew down in an arc.

I jumped into the first trench; rushing around the next corner, I collided with an English officer in an open jacket and a drooping cravat. Forgoing the use of the pistol, I seized him by the throat and hurled him against a stack of sandbags, before which he collapsed. Behind me appeared the head of an old major, who shouted to me, "Beat that dog to death!" I left this work to those who followed, turned to the lower trench, which was swarming with Englishmen, and fired my pistol at them with such zeal that after the last shot I must have pulled the trigger ten more times. A man next to me was throwing hand grenades among the men hurrying away. A plate-shaped steel helmet rose, gyrating high into the air.

In a minute the battle was decided. The English jumped out of their trenches and fled in battalions across the open field. From the crest of the embankment, terrific pursuit fire ensued. The fleeing men somersaulted as they ran, and in a few seconds the ground was covered with corpses. Only a few escaped.

I snatched the rifle out of the hand of a sergeant who was gawking at this spectacle with his mouth open. My first victim was an Englishman whom I shot down at one hundred and fifty meters between two Germans. He collapsed like a folding knife and remained lying there.

After all the work was done, we continued onwards. Success had inflamed the attacking spirit and bravado of each individual to a white heat. There was no longer any question of leading unified units. Nevertheless, every man knew only one slogan: "Forward!" Everyone ran straight ahead.

As a target I chose a small hill on which the debris of a cottage, a grave cross and a destroyed airplane could be seen. My stubborn rush forward led me into the middle of a wall of flames of our own mobile barrage. I had to throw myself into a crater to take cover and wait for the fire to advance further. Next to me I discovered a young officer from another regiment who, like me, was all alone rejoicing in the success of that first assault. In those few minutes, the shared enthusiasm brought us as close as if we had known each other for years. The next jump separated us forever.

Next to the ruined house was a small trench. I jumped in at a run and found it unoccupied. Immediately afterwards Lieutenants Kius and von Wedelstädt appeared. One of von Wedelstädt's orderlies, who was the last to arrive, collapsed in the middle of the jump and remained dead, having been hit through the eye. When Wedelstädt saw the last soldier of his company fall, he leaned his head on the trench wall and wept. He, too, would not survive the day.

Basically, there was a strongly fortified trench position with two machine gun nests at both ends. The barrage had already passed beyond that position; the enemy seemed to have recovered and was firing at full force. We were separated from him by a five hundred meter wide strip of terrain over which the torrents of bullets buzzed like swarms of bees.

After a short pause to catch our breath, we jumped out of our trench section towards the enemy with a few men. It was a matter of life and death. After a few jumps, I was alone with an escort facing the machine gun nest on the left. Behind a small lump of earth, I saw a flat helmeted head beside a thin column of rising steam. I approached by very short jumps in order not to give time for him to aim. Each time I lay on the ground, the man would shoot an entire magazine at me, with which I fired a series of well-aimed shots. "Ammo, ammo!" I turned to see him lying on his side, twisting in agony.

When I think back today to that blind run across an open field against a position with such a strong resistance, I must confess that we were possessed by a rather unbelievable audacity. And yet, where would success in war be if the rush to action did not seize individuals and propel them forward in an irresistible momentum? Sometimes it seemed to me that even death was afraid to step in their way.

From the left, where the resistance was a little less strong, some men appeared who could almost reach the defenders with hand grenades. I took the last leap and stumbled over a wire entanglement into the trench. The Englishmen, caught under fire from all sides, fled to the machine gun nest on the right, leaving their weapons on the ground. The machine gun was half hidden under a huge pile of fired casings. It was still red-hot and steaming. In front of it laid an athletic English corpse who had had one of his eyes plucked out by a shot to the head, which was my doing. The giant guy with the big white eyeball in front of his skull looked chilling. Since I was almost pining away from thirst, I didn't linger but looked for water. A tunnel entrance attracted me. I looked in and saw a man sitting below, pulling ammunition belts over his knees and arranging them. Instead of taking him down immediately, as prudence dictated, I called out to him beforehand, "Come here, hands up!" He jumped up, stared at me in bewilderment, and disappeared into the darkness of the tunnel. He probably fell victim to the hand grenade I hurled at him seconds later.

At last, I discovered a tin box full of cooling water. I gulped down the oily liquid in long gulps, filled an English canteen and also gave a drink to the other comrades who suddenly filled the trench.

Meanwhile, the machine gun nest on the right and the trench sixty meters in front of us were still putting up a fierce resistance. We tried to bring the English machine gun to bear, but were unsuccessful; rather, in this effort a bullet whizzed past my head, grazed a hunter lieutenant standing behind me, and wounded a man very seriously in the thigh. With more luck, the operator of a light machine gun brought his weapon into position at the edge of our small crescent trench and fired a series of projectiles into the flank of the English.

This moment of surprise was used by the assault troops on the right: they ran head-on into the trench, in front of our still quite intact 9th Company, under the leadership of Lieutenant Gipkens. Rifle-wielding figures suddenly rose from all craters and, with wide eyes and foaming mouths, ran with a terrible roar of hurrah against the enemy position, from which the defenders emerged by the hundreds with their hands raised.

Pardon was not given. The Englishmen, arms raised, rushed to the rear through the first wave of the storm, where the fury of battle had not yet risen to such a boiling heat. Gipkens' orderly put down probably a dozen of them with his thirty two-round repeating pistol.

I cannot blame our men for this bloodthirsty behavior. Killing a defenseless man is a vile act. During the war, no one was more disgusting to me than the heroes of the regulars' table, who told the well-known story of the Bavarians and the prisoner transport with a slimy laugh: "Have you heard the story about the lash? Delicious!"

On the other hand, a defender, who chases his bullets through the body of the attacker up to five steps, has to bear the consequences. The fighter, who had a bloody veil flowing in front of his eyes during the run-up, can no longer change his feelings. He does not want to capture; he wants to kill. He has lost sight of any goal and is under the spell of violent primal urges. Only when blood has flowed does the fog leave his brain; he looks around as if awakening from a heavy dream. Only then is he a modern soldier again, able to solve a new tactical task.

This is the state we found ourselves in after conquering the trench. A crowd of men had gathered and were standing, shouting among themselves, in mass. Officers showed them the extension of the trench, and the huge belligerent heap of men started moving with astonishing indifference, ponderously.

The trench ran out to a height where some enemy columns began to appear. We advanced, stopping and firing from time to time, until we were blocked by heavy fire. It was a most embarrassing sensation to hear the bullets slam into the ground beside our heads. Kius, who also came over, picked up a flattened bullet that had stopped half a meter from his nose. We used a short break to reach one of the craters that had already become rare here. A crowd of officers from our battalion, now led by Lieutenant Lindenberg, gathered there, since unfortunately the Baron von Solemacher had also received a deadly hit. On the right slope of the ravine, Lieutenant Breyer, commander of the 10th Hunters Regiment, strolled through the machine gun fire, to the general amusement, with his walking stick in his hand and a long green hunter's whistle in his mouth, as if he were on a hare hunt.

We told each other briefly of our previous adventures and offered each other canteens and chocolate, then moved forward again by "general request." The enemy machine guns, apparently threatened in the flank, had disappeared. We may have gained three to four kilometers so far. The path was swarming with storm troops. Behind us, as far as the eye could see, the troops of the line were advancing in rows or columns. Unfortunately, we were far too close; fortunately, during the storm, we did not realize how many men we had left behind.

Finding no resistance, we reached the hill. To our right, some khaki figures jumped out of a trench section. Most of them were knocked down. The hill was fortified by a series of dugouts. The swelling clouds of smoke coming out of the entrances revealed that our men, as they passed, threw hand grenades into them, flooding them with smoke; often the occupants came out with their arms raised and their knees shaking. The canteen and cigarettes were taken from them and they were shown the direction to the rear, where they fled at great speed. One young Englishman had already surrendered to me when he suddenly turned and disappeared back into his dugout. Since he was hiding down below despite my orders to come out, we put an end to his hesitation with some hand grenades and moved on. A narrow footpath disappeared beyond the high ground. A signpost said that it led to Vraucourt. While the others lingered near the dugouts, I climbed the hill with Lieutenant Heins.

On the other side of the valley laid the ruins of the village of Vraucourt. In front of it, mussel flashes of a firing battery could be seen, whose operators fled into the village at the sight of the first storm wave. The crew of a row of dugouts built into a narrow walkway also rushed out and escaped. I shot one of them down the moment he jumped out of the entrance closest to me.

With two men of my company, who had reported to me in the meantime, I proceeded along the narrow path. To the right of it laid an occupied position from which we received heavy fire. We withdrew into the first dugout, above which the bullets of both parties soon crossed. In front of it laid my Englishman, a bloody young fellow whom my shot had hit right through the side of the skull. It was a peculiar feeling to look a man in the eye whom I had killed myself.

We were not disturbed by the growing fire, but settled into the dugout and ate up the food left behind, as our stomachs reminded us that we had not yet enjoyed anything during the entire attack. We found ham, white bread, jam and a stone jug full of ginger liquor. After fortifying myself, I sat down on an empty cookie tin and read some English magazines teeming with rather distasteful outbursts against "the Huns." Gradually we got bored with the situation and returned in leaps and bounds to the beginning of the path, where a crowd of men had gathered. From there, we saw a battalion of the 164th Regiment coming from the left near Vraucourt. We decided to storm the village and hurried forward again through the path. Just before we reached the edge of the village, our own artillery, which continued to fire dully at the same spot until morning, set us as a target. A heavy shell struck in the middle of the path and tore four of our men apart. The others retreated unharmed.

As I learned later, the artillery had orders to continue firing at maximum range. This incomprehensibly stupid order snatched the most beautiful fruits of victory from our hands. Gritting our teeth, we had to stop in front of the wall of fire.

To seek a gap in the fire, we turned further to the right, where just then a company commander of 76th Infantry Regiment was preparing to storm the Vraucourt position. We joined in with hurrahs, but we had scarcely broken through when our artillery shot us out again. Three times we stormed and three times we had to turn back. Cursing, we occupied some craters, where a fire in the meadow, caused by the shells, in which many wounded died, became extraordinarily annoying to us. Moreover, some bullets from an English rifle killed a few more of our men.

Slowly, dusk fell. In places, the rifle fire blazed up once again, only to gradually die out. The exhausted troops looked for a place to spend the night. Officers shouted their names incessantly to rally the fragmented companies.

Twelve men of the 7th Company had gathered around me during the last hour; as it was beginning to get cold, I led them to the small dugout in front of which my Englishman laid and sent them out to collect some blankets and coats of the fallen men. When I had accommodated them all, I gave way to my curiosity, which drove me into the artillery trough ahead. I took Fusilier Haller with me, whom I trusted to have the greatest sporting spirit. We advanced, rifles ready to fire, toward the trench on which our artillery fire was still heaving, and first examined a dugout which had apparently been recently abandoned by English artillery officers. On a table was a huge gramophone, which Haller immediately set in motion. The merry couplet purring from the cylinder gave me a macabre feeling. I threw the box on the floor, where it spat out a few more buzzing sounds like a slain man and fell silent. The shelter was extremely comfortably furnished; even a small fireplace, on whose ledge pipes and tobacco lay, with armchairs placed around in a circle. Merry old England! We did not force ourselves, of course, but took what we liked. I picked out a haversack, linen, a small metal bottle full of whiskey, a map case, and some wondrous Roger and Gallet toiletries, presumably tender mementos of a Parisian furlough.

An adjoining room contained a kitchen, the supplies of which we gazed at in awe. There was a whole crate full of raw eggs, of which we immediately sucked down a considerable number, since we hardly remembered that such things still existed. On the wall shelves were piled cans of meat, cans of delicious thickened jam, bottles of coffee essence, tomatoes and onions; in short, everything the gourmet could wish for.

I often remembered this sight later, when we laid in the trenches for weeks on end with meager portions of bread, watery soups and thin jam. The German field soldier, in a worn-out coat, worse fed than a Chinese chicken coup, hurried for four years from battlefield to battlefield, in order to make his iron fist felt again and again by the opponents, who were many times superior in number, well-equipped and well-fed. There is no greater sign of the power of the idea that propelled us. To walk towards death, to die in moments of enthusiasm, is a lot; to starve and to die for one's cause is much more.

After this little insight into the enemy's economic conditions, we left the dugout and strode into the trench where we found two sparkling new abandoned guns. I took a clay stone and drew the number of my company on them. Then, with our own artillery still continually shooting iron around our ears, we returned to the others.

Our front line, by now formed by straggling troops, was two hundred meters behind us. I placed two sentries in front of the dugout and ordered the others to keep their rifles in their hands. After I had arranged the relief, ate some food and noted down the day's experiences in short bullet points, I fell asleep.

At 1 o'clock, we were awakened by the sound of hurrah and brisk fire to our right. We grabbed our rifles, rushed out of the room and positioned ourselves in a large crater. A few scattered Germans came back from the front and were fired upon from our line. Two of them were left lying on the road. Warned by this incident, we waited until the commotion behind us had died down, made ourselves known by shouting and went back into our own line. There sat the leader of the 2nd Company, Lieutenant Kosik, who was wounded in the arm and also could not speak a word because of a severe cold that afflicted him, with about sixty from the 73rd Regiment. Since he had to go back to the first-aid post, I took command of his squad, which included three officers. In addition, there were two companies from the regiment, Gipkens and Vorbeck, which were also mixed together.

The battalion commander was Captain Freiherr von Ledebour and the regimental commander was now Major Dietlein, since Major von Bardeleben had already retired that the morning due to an injury.

I spent the rest of the night together with some NCOs of the 2nd Company in a small hole in the ground, where we froze from the cold. In the morning I had breakfast from the captured supplies and sent people to Quéant to get coffee and food from the kitchen. Our own artillery began its accursed firing again, and as a first morning salute put a direct hit on us in a crater that housed four men of the Machine Gun Company. In the first twilight, a platoon leader of my company, the vice sergeant Kumpart, joined me with a few more men.

I had scarcely got the night cold out of my system when I was ordered to storm the Vraucourt position, which had already been partially taken, with the remnants of the 76th Regiment on my right. We moved in the dense morning fog to the staging area, a high ground south of Ecoust where many of the previous day's dead lay. There was, as usual when unclear attack orders are received, a tremendous commotion among the storm leaders, which was only ended by the sheaf of an enemy machine gun. Everyone jumped into the nearest craters except for Sergeant Kumpart, who laid moaning. I rushed to him with a medic, pulled him into a crater and bandaged him up. He had received a heavy shot to the knee. We removed several pieces of bone from the wound with pliers. He died a few days later. The case was particularly close to my heart because Kumpart had been my drill sergeant three years ago in Recouvrence.

In a discussion with Captain von Ledebour, I explained the futility of a frontal assault, since the Vraucourt position, already partly in our possession, could be rolled up from the left with much less loss. We decided not to carry out the attack, and the result showed that we had made the right decision.

On such occasions, the establishment of the far-behind command posts of the higher leadership, the necessity of which is, of course, clear to me, took its revenge. However, such orders clearly betrayed a lack of front-line experience. The days of the unprepared frontal attack are gone forever. The common man, to whom the enemy guns dictated the law of action, could not fall for such errors. It occurred only where the enemy was weak. The strong parts of the position then fell of their own accord. . . .

For the time being, we settled into the craters on the high ground. Gradually the sun broke through, and English planes appeared, machine-gunning our holes, but were soon driven away by our own planes. From the valley of Ecoust, a battery climbed up to take position, an unusual sight for old trench warriors; but it was immediately shot up. A single horse broke loose and galloped through the terrain; a ghostly sight, this animal gone mad on a wide, lonely expanse, under shifting clouds of bullets. The enemy airplanes had just disappeared when the first shots came. First some shrapnel bursts, then numerous light and heavy caliber shells fell. We laid as if on a platter. Several anxious minds added fuel to the fire by running headlong back and forth instead of crouching in their craters to let the blessing wash over them. In such situations, one must be a fatalist. I took this principle to heart by eating the downright magnificent contents of a captured can full of gooseberry jam. Thus, slowly, it became noon.

Movement had been observed on the left of the Vraucourt position for quite some time. Now we saw just in front of us the arc-shaped trajectory and the white impact of German stick hand grenades. The moment had come.

I ordered the advance. Without receiving any stronger fire, we reached the enemy trench and jumped in, joyfully greeted by an assault squad of 76th Regiment. In the developing hand grenade attack, we proceeded slowly, similar to Cambrai. Unfortunately, the enemy artillery did not fail to notice that we were slowly eating our way through their lines. A sharp fire assault of shrapnel and light shells fell in front of us, but it fell mainly on the reinforcements that were flowing, in the open, towards the trench. We endeavored to deal with the enemy as quickly as possible in order to undermine the fire.

The Vraucourt position seemed to have been still under construction, for some pieces of the trench were only indicated by lifting off the turf. When we jumped over such a piece, all the fire of the perimeter was concentrated on us. Likewise, we took the enemy rushing across these spots in front of us under fire, so that the short outlined sections were soon piled with corpses. It was a nerve-wracking chase. We hurried past the still warm, stocky figures, under whose short skirts strong knees shone, or crawled over them. They were Scottish highlanders, and the nature of the resistance showed that we had no cowards before us.

After gaining a few hundred meters in this way, hand and rifle grenades falling ever more densely gave us pause. The men began to give way.

"The Tommy is making a counterpunch!"

"I just want to make contact!"

"Hand grenades forward; hand grenades, hand grenades!"

"Lieutenant, watch out!"

It is in trench warfare, where fighting is most brutal, that such setbacks are most common. The bravest rush forward, shooting and throwing. The masses follow on their heels as a will-less herd. As they clash, the fighters leap back and forth to avoid the devastating throws, bumping into those pushing after them. Only the foremost overlook the situation; further back, wild panic breaks out among the crowd wedged in the narrow trench. If the enemy recognizes the moment, all is lost; now the leader must show whether he wears the epaulets rightly, although the well-known "queasy" feeling creeps over him.

I managed to gather a handful of men with whom I formed a resistance nest behind a wide parapet. At a few meters, we exchanged projectiles with an invisible opponent. It took courage to hold my head high during the slamming impacts while the sand of the parapet whipped up. A 76er next to me, with a wild look on his face and no thought of cover, fired one round after another until he collapsed covered in blood. A bullet had pierced his forehead with the thud of a board hitting the ground. He crumpled in the corner of his trench and remained in a crouching position, leaning his head against the trench wall. His blood flowed, as if poured from a bucket, onto the bottom of the trench. His gurgled breathing sounded at longer and longer intervals and finally ceased altogether. I seized his rifle and continued firing. At last a little pause occurred. Two men who had been ahead made an attempt to jump back over cover. One fell dead into the trench with a shot to the head, the other could only reach it by crawling because of a shot to the stomach.

We sat waiting on the trench bottom, smoking English cigarettes. Now and then well-aimed rifle grenades arrowed their way over. The wounded man with the bullet in his belly, a bloody young man, laid between us, stretching almost comfortably like a cat in the warm rays of the setting sun. He was slipping away into death with a childish smile. It was a sight in which there was nothing gloomy or unpleasant, but only a clear feeling of affection for the dying man touched me. Even the moans of his companion became more and more faint.

Several times, crouching low in the outlined places over the corpses of the highlanders, we tried to advance further, but were driven back again and again by machine-gun fire and rifle grenades. Every hit I saw was fatal. Thus the front part of the trench gradually filled up with corpses; in return we constantly received reinforcements from the rear. Soon there was a light or heavy machine gun behind each parapet. I too took my place behind one of those guns and fired until the forefinger of my right hand was blackened by smoke. When the cooling water had evaporated, the boxes were passed around and filled with the most natural of procedures, amidst everyone's unsympathetic jokes.

The sun was low on the horizon. It seemed that the second day of the battle was now over. I took a close look at the surroundings for the first time and sent a report and sketch to the rear. Our trench intersected the Vraucourt-Mory road at a distance of five hundred meters, which was veiled by cloth screens attached to the trees. Along a slope, on the rear, some enemy detachments ran across the field on which bullets were hailing. The cloudless evening sky was crossed by a squadron in black-white-red colors. The last rays of the sun, already setting behind the horizon, colored it like a flock of flamingos in a beautiful, subtle pink. We unfolded our field maps and laid out the white reverse side to indicate to our airmen how far we had penetrated the enemy.

A cool evening wind heralded a harsh night. I was leaning against the trench wall, wrapped in an English overcoat, and talking to little Schultz, the companion of my Indian patrol, who, like a good comrade, had always appeared at the most precarious moments, this time with four heavy machine guns. Men of all companies with young, sharp-cut faces sat under their steel helmets at the sentry posts. Their commanders had fallen; they were taking up their positions alone and in the most opportune place.

Then hand grenades rang out again from the right and German flares went up on the left. From somewhere a faint, many-voiced hurrah fluttered over with the wind. It ignited. "They've gone around, they've gone around!" In one of those moments of enthusiasm that precede great deeds, everyone grabbed their rifles and charged forward in the trench. After a brief hand grenade skirmish, a squad of Highlanders rushed toward the road. Now there was no stopping them. Despite warning shouts: "Be careful, the machine gun on the left is still firing!" we jumped out of the trench and had reached the road in no time, which was swarming with distraught highlanders. A long, dense wire entanglement prevented their escape to the rear, so that they had to run past us at a distance of fifty meters like trapped big game under thunderous cheering and rapid fire. Rapidly mounted machine guns made the slaughter devastating.

Cursing with a jammed bullet that prevented me from shooting, I turned as a result of a blow to the shoulder, and looked into the rage-distorted face of little Schultz: "They are still shooting, the cursed swine!" I followed his hand movement and saw a number of figures in a small network of trenches, separated from us by the road, half of them loading, the other half with their rifle at their cheeks. Already the first hand grenades were flying from the right, flinging a Scotsman's torso high into the air.

Reason dictated that I remain in my place and calmly finish off the opponents with a few shots. Instead, I threw away my rifle and rushed into the street with clenched fists between the two parties. Unfortunately, I was still wearing my English coat and my red-brimmed field cap. In the midst of the elation of victory I felt a sharp blow on the left side of my chest; darkness fell around me. Gone! I thought for sure that I had been hit in the heart, but I felt neither pain nor fear in anticipation of my immediate death. Since, to my astonishment, I did not collapse and did not discover a hole in my shirt, I turned back to the enemy. A man of my company rushed up to me: "Mr. Lieutenant, take that coat off!" and tore the dangerous garment from my shoulder.

A new hurrah went through the air. From the right, where hand grenades had been used all afternoon, a number of Germans jumped across the road to help, led by a young officer in brown Manchester. It was Kius. The Scots were annihilated by rifle fire and hand grenades in a few moments of fury. The road was completely covered with corpses, while the few survivors fled in pursuit of our fire.

As I stood in the captured trench section, talking with Kius, I felt a damp sensation on my chest. Tearing off my blouse, I saw that I had received a shot across the heart. The bullet had passed just under my Iron Cross, leaving two holes in my shirt and two in my body. No doubt one of our men (I strongly suspected the one who tore off my coat) had mistaken me for an Englishman and shot me at a point blank range.

Kius put a bandage on me and could only move me with difficulty to leave the battlefield at this exciting moment. We parted with a: "See you in Hannover!"

I chose a companion on the sharply shelled roadway, looked for my map case, in which my war diary was tucked, and went back through the trench in which we had fought our way forward.

Our battle cry had been so tremendous that the enemy artillery abruptly went into action. The ground behind the road, but above all, the trench, was hit by a very intense barrage. Since the wound I had already sustained seemed more than enough, I moved in leaps and bounds, from parapet to parapet.

Suddenly, at the edge of the trench next to me, there was a deafening crash. I received a blow to the back of the skull and fell forward, stunned. When I awoke, I was hanging upside down over the slide of a heavy machine gun, staring down at the bottom of the trench into an alarmingly rapidly expanding pool of red. The blood gushed out so inexorably that I thought it was impossible to get away. Since my companion claimed not to see any brains yet, I pulled myself up and ran on. Here I had the receipt for my carelessness, to go without a steel helmet into the fight.

Despite the double loss of blood, I was tremendously excited and, as if possessed by a fixed idea, implored everyone I met in the trench to rush forward and join the fight. Soon we had escaped the zone of light field guns and slowed our pace.

On the path of Noreuil, I passed the brigade command post, reported to Major General Höbel, to whom I reported our success, and asked to come to the aid of the storm troops with reserves. The general told me that I had been pronounced dead at the command posts since yesterday. It was not the first time that such a thing had happened to me in the war.

In Noreuil, close to the road, a tall stack of crates full of hand grenades was on fire. We hurried past it with very mixed feelings. Behind the village a driver took me on his empty ammunition wagon. I had a lively discussion with the leader of the truck who wanted to have the two wounded Englishmen, who had supported me during the last part of the journey, thrown out of the truck.

The traffic was incredibly dense on the Noreuil-Quéant road. Those who did not see it cannot form a picture of the endless columns that belong to a great offensive. Behind Quéant, the throng grew again and assumed fantastic proportions. I turned to one of the traffic officers, identifiable by white bandages, who directed me to a place in a passenger car to the Sauchy-Cauchy field hospital. We had to wait for over half an hour as nested wagons and automobiles blocked the way. The doctors in the operating room of the field hospital were feverishly busy; nevertheless, the surgeon marveled at the fortunate nature of my injuries. Even the head wound had entry and exit without even touching the top of the skull.

After I had slept excellently during the night, I was transported the next morning to the Cantin infirmary, where, to my delight, I met Lieutenant Sprenger, whom I had not seen since the beginning of the storm. He had been wounded in the thigh by a rifle shot.

After a short stay in the Bavarian field hospital of Montigny, we were loaded onto a hospital train in Douai and traveled to Berlin, where my sixth double wound healed in fifteen days, as perfectly as the others.

Unfortunately, I learned in Hannover that among many other acquaintances, little Schultz had fallen during the melee attack. Kius had come out with a minor stomach wound. Whoever observed our reunion in a small Hanoverian bar would hardly have thought that we had parted only two weeks ago to music other than the peaceful bang of billiards balls.

XVIII

English Advances

ON June 4, 1918, I rejoined the regiment, which was at rest near the village of Vraucourt, now far behind the front. The new commander, Major von Lüttichau, gave me the command of my old 7th Company.

As I approached the quarters, my men ran to meet me, took my things, and welcomed me in triumph. It was as if I had returned to the bosom of a family.

We lived in a cluster of corrugated iron huts in the middle of an overgrown meadow landscape, from whose greenery countless yellow flowers shimmered. The desolate terrain, which we had christened "Wallachia," was populated by herds of grazing horses. When one stepped outside the door of the huts, one felt that frightening sense of emptiness that sometimes grips the cowboy, the Bedouin, and every other inhabitant of the desert. In the evening we took long walks around the barracks, looking for partridge nests or war material hidden in the grass. One afternoon I rode to the valley near Vraucourt, so hard-fought two months ago, and the edges of which were strewn with grave crosses. I found many familiar names.

Soon the regiment received orders to occupy the front line of the position lying in front of the village of Puisieux-au-Mont. We made a night drive on trucks to Achiet-le-Grand. We often had to stop when the cones of parachute bombs falling from night bombing planes lifted the white ribbon of the road out of the darkness. Near or far, the multiple whistles of heavy explosive shells were engulfed by the rolling thuds of the impacts. Then the uncertain arms of the searchlights scanned the dark sky for the treacherous night birds, shrapnel sprayed like elegant toys, and flares chased one after another in long chains like fiery wolves.

A persistent smell of corpses lingered over the conquered area, sometimes more, sometimes less intense, but always exciting the nerves and enveloping them in a mood of grotesque and foreboding eeriness.

"Offensive perfume," the voice of a cynical old warrior rang out next to me. We seemed to be passing through a series of mass graves. We walked along the railroad embankment from Achiet-le-Grand, leading to Bapaume and then across the fields towards the position. The fire was lively. As we rested for a moment, two medium caliber shells struck beside us. The memory of the unforgettable night of terror on March 19th drove us forward. Close behind the front line there was a noisy, detached company, which was just about to pass us when they had their mouths shut by several dozen shrapnel shells. With a hail of curse words, my men plunged headlong into the nearest running trench. Three men from my company had to return to the medical shelter with severe bleeding.

At 3 o'clock, I arrived, completely exhausted, in my dugout, whose irritating confinement held out the prospect of a series of unhappy days.

The reddish light of a candle glowed amidst an indescribable cloud of haze. I stumbled over a tangle of legs and brought life to the place with the incantation "Relief!" A string of curses escaped from an oven-shaped hole, then, gradually, out came an unshaven face, a pair of battered epaulets, a weathered uniform, and two blocks of mud in which boots were probably attached. We sat down together at the makeshift table and performed the business of the hand over, each trying to bully the other for a dozen iron portions and some flare guns. Then my predecessor squeezed his way out through the narrow tunnel neck into the open with the prophecy that the "sinkhole" would not hold for another three days. I remained behind as the new commander of Section A.

The position, which I had inspected the following morning, offered little to be pleased about. Right in front of the dugout I encountered two bleeding coffee-carriers who had been hit by a shrapnel barrage on their approach. A few steps further, Fusilier A. signed off with a ricochet shot.

We had the village of Bucquoy in front of us and Puisieux-au-Mont in our rear. The company laid, unstaggered, in the flat, narrow, front line and was separated from 76th Infantry Regiment on the right by a large, unoccupied gap. The left wing of the regimental section included a chopped-up little patch of forest, Copse 125. In accordance with the orders, no tunnels had been dug. The men were housed two by two in small holes in the ground covered with armored plates, what we called "Siegfried plates."

My first order of business was to find myself a new shelter, since my current dugout was located behind a completely different section. A hut-like structure that I found in a dilapidated trench section seemed quite suitable, especially after whipping it into shape by dragging in several ordnance instruments. Together with my lad, I led the life of a hermit in the countryside, disturbed only occasionally by messengers and orderlies who carried the cumbersome paperwork, even into this remote cave. Drawings and frequent appointment messages provided us with a variety of necessary distractions. One always had so much to do with the internal organization that one could hardly take care of the tactical trifles. One was also asked little about it. Often the cartridge case that had been thrown away seemed far more important. Every time I was notified of a revising superior, I ran through the trench, picked up paper and cartridge cases, and instructed the guards about how to report and click their heels properly. They were also instructed to never commit the crime of turning their faces away from the enemy trench, and to not put down their rifles. Three days of arrest were an unconditional tax for these offenses.

These rules did great harm. The form stifled the spirit. The war became bureaucratized. Meanwhile, the front line lieutenant had far too much discipline in his bones to bring up what was cursed in every platoon leader's dugout, before and after sipping the schnapps. Nevertheless, he was the one called upon to merge the old Prussian spirit with the evolving forms of modern warfare.

But back to my shelter, which I had given the beautiful name "Wahnfried Villa." The only gripe I had was the cover, which was only relatively bombproof, that is, only as long as no shells hit it directly. However, I consoled myself with the thought that I was in no better a position than my men. Every noon my lad would lay out a blanket for me in a giant crater to which we had dug a passage to and set up as a sunbathing area. More often, however, my siesta was disturbed by shells hitting nearby or the falling fragments of anti-aircraft shrapnel.

The front line suffered relatively little from enemy fire; otherwise it would have soon become untenable. Puisieux and the neighboring valleys, however, were under constant bombardment, which, in the evening hours, became extraordinarily dense. Food recovery and relief were thus very much compromised.

At 2 a.m. on June 14th, I was relieved by Kius, who had also returned and was leading the 2nd Company. We spent our rest time on the railroad embankment at Achiet-le-Grand, under the protection of our barracks and dugouts. The Englishman frequently subjected us to heavy railroad fire, to which, among others, the regular sergeant of the 3rd Company, Rackebrand, fell victim. A few days earlier a terrible accident had occurred. An airman dropped his bomb in the middle of the chapel where the 76th Infantry Regiment was located. The chapel was also surrounded by a crowd of soldiers from other regiments. Many men from the 73rd were also among those who were hit.

In the immediate vicinity of the railroad embankment laid a number of shot-up tanks, which I inspected with interest on my walks. Some of them bore mocking, threatening or auspicious names and war paint, but they were all badly battered. The narrow, bullet-ridden tank cockpit with its tangle of pipes, rods and wires must have been an extremely uncomfortable place to be in during a storm, when those behemoths, to escape the artillery shots, had to meander across the Walstatt like clumsy, giant beetles. I thought vividly of the men who were locked inside those fiery furnaces.

On the morning of June 18th, the 7th Company had to return to Puisieux because of the uncertain situation, in order to be at the disposal of the K. T. K. for carrying material and tactical use. We moved into the cellars and tunnels lying on the outskirts of Bucquoy. Just as we arrived, a group of heavy shells pounded the surrounding gardens. Nevertheless, I was not deterred from having breakfast in a small arbor in front of the entrance to my shelter. After a while the shells roared in again. I threw myself down. Flames rose up right next to me. A medic of my company standing nearby, who was passing by with some cooking utensils full of water, collapsed after being hit in the abdomen. We bandaged him up while large drops of sweat appeared on his forehead. As I tried to comfort him, he moaned out, "The shot is fatal, I feel it very clearly." In spite of this prophecy, I was able to shake his hand half a year later when he arrived in Hanover.

In the afternoon, I took a lonely walk through Puisieux, which was completely destroyed. The village had already been hammered into a heap of rubble during the summer battles. Craters and the remains of walls were covered with a dense foliage, from which the white discs of the ruin-friendly elder shone everywhere. Numerous fresh shell impacts had completely removed the top soil and laid bare anew the earth of the gardens, which had already been turned over so many times.

The village street was lined with the remnants of war, which were to be used in an advance that had come to a sudden halt. Shot-up wagons, discarded ammunition, melee ordnance, and decaying horses, buffeted by swarms of flies, proclaimed the nothingness of all things in the struggle for life. The church, which once stood on the highest point of the village, was no more than a heap of stones. While I was picking a bouquet of beautiful roses overgrown with wild flowers, the nearby impact of shells warned me to be careful on this dance floor of death.

After a few days we relieved the 9th Company in the main line of resistance, which was about five hundred meters behind the front line. In the process, three men of my company were wounded. The following morning, near my dugout, Captain von Ledebour was wounded in the foot by a shrapnel bullet. Even though he was severely lung-sick, he felt strongly that his purpose was to stay on battlefield with his men. He ended up succumbing to the minor wound. He died a few days later in the field hospital. On the 28th, the leader of my ration carriers was hit by a shell fragment. This was the ninth loss in my company within a very short period of time.

After a week in the front line, we had to occupy the main line of resistance once again, since our relief battalion was almost disbanded by the Spanish flu. Several of our own men also reported sick every day. In the neighboring division, the flu raged so strongly that an enemy aircraft dropped leaflets saying that the English would take over the relief if the troops were not withdrawn immediately. But we learned that the flu epidemic was spreading just as ravenously on their side as it was on ours. In our case, the poor rations were exacerbating the situation. At the same time, we were constantly on high alert, since Copse 125 was continually being bombarded by maximum shelling. As a result of the gases released by the explosions, part of the 6th Company had fallen ill with carbon monoxide poisoning. Equipped with oxygen apparatuses, we had to go into all of the dugouts and bring the men out, many of whom were unconscious.

One afternoon, while walking through my section, I found several buried boxes full of English ammunition and, in my recklessness, blew off the top of my right index finger while attempting to disassemble a rifle grenade. That same evening, while I was standing on the cover of my dugout with Lieutenant Sprenger, a heavy shell exploded nearby. We argued about the distance, which Sprenger estimated at ten meters, I estimated it to be closer to thirty meters. To see how far I could trust my information in this regard, I measured and found the crater to be twenty two meters from our location. One is easily inclined to underestimate the distance.

On July 20th, I was in Puisieux again with my company. I stood on a half destroyed wall all afternoon and observed the battle scene, which made a very suspicious impression on me.

Copse 125 was often enveloped in thick smoke, due to the constant powerful bursts of fire, while green and red flares rose and fell incessantly. Sometimes the artillery fire was silent, and then one could hear the crackling of a few machine guns and the dull bang of distant hand grenades. The whole thing looked almost like a graceful game from my vantage point. It lacked the violence of a large-scale battle, and yet one could feel the bitter struggle between two iron forces. . . .

From the empty, wide terrain, the eyes of a thousand hidden men stare at the small patch of forest, from which brown columns of earth can be seen dancing around the tops of the falling oak trees. In the depths of the perimeter, in trenches, craters, caves and ruins, men and material stagger, waiting to be deployed against the chopped-up copse.

Far back at two opposite poles, two generals sit at map-covered tables. A report, a short lecture, a few sentences to an orderly officer, a telephone conversation. An hour later, the lightning of a new burst of fire erupts in the old craters, a fresh human hecatomb bleeds to death in stuffy smoke. . . .

Towards evening I was called by the readiness commander, where I learned that the enemy had penetrated our trench system on the left wing. In order to create a little apron for us again, it was ordered that Lieutenant Petersen with the assault company should clear the Hedge Trench, while I, with my men, would do the same to an approach path running parallel to it in a valley. We set off at dawn, but received such heavy infantry fire in our initial assault position that we abandoned the plan for the time being. I had the Elbinger Path occupied and made up for the missed night's sleep in a huge cave tunnel. At 11 a.m., I was awakened by the sound of hand grenades from the left wing, where we were manning a barricade. I hurried over and found the usual picture of barricade fighting. At the entrenchment, white hand grenade clouds swirled, while two machine gunners on each side of the parapet rattled off round after round. In between, men crouched, jumping back and forth. The Englishman's little coup d'état had already been beaten off, but it had cost us a man who laid behind the barricade, torn apart by hand grenade fragments.

Towards evening, I was ordered to lead the company back to Puisieux, where on arrival I found the order to participate with two groups in the rolling up of the trench in the valley the next morning. We set out at 3:40 a.m. to the initial position, that is, Lieutenant Voigt of the assault company with a shock troop and I, with my two groups.

We had orders to split the trench after a five-minute artillery and mine preparation from Red Point K to Red Point Z1.

I must not conceal the fact that we both considered the fire preparation and, in general, the taking and occupation of the trench lying deep in the valley, to be unnecessary and wrong. The decisive point was the Hedge Trench; if one wanted to attack, one had to take it and was then also in possession of the valley. I had the definite suspicion that the attack was ordered from behind according to the map, because whoever had the terrain in front of his eyes could not possibly create such orders.

After the preparation, during which one of our men was wounded, we stepped up and rolled up the trench. Just before Z1 we encountered resistance, which was broken by hand grenades. Since we had reached our objective and were not eager for further fighting, we built a barricade and left a group with a machine gun behind it.

The only pleasure I got out of it was the behavior of the storm troopers, who reminded me vividly of Grimmelshausen's Simplisissimus. These young warriors with shaggy hair and puttees got into a heated argument twenty meters in front of the enemy because one of them had scolded the other one, cursing like country servants. "Man, not everyone is as scared as you are!" one of them shouted at last and rolled up another fifty meters of trench all by himself.

In the afternoon, the barricade group fell back. They had suffered losses and could not hold on any longer. I had already given up on the men and was surprised that anyone at all had been able to pass through the long line of the valley trench in the daylight and come out of it alive. These are the consequences of the paper war.

Despite our counterattacks, the enemy sat firmly in the left wing of our forward line and in the barricaded lines of communication, threatening the main line of resistance.

On July 24th, I went for orientation to the new Section C of the main resistance line, which I was to take over the following day. I had the company commander, Lieutenant Gipkens, show me the barricade at the Hedge Trench and sat down next to him on a post. Suddenly Gipkens grabbed me and yanked me aside. A split second later a projectile splattered apart on the sand of my post. By a lucky coincidence, he had observed a rifle being slowly pushed out of an embrasure in the enemy barricade forty meters away, thus saving my life through his keen artist's eyes. As I was told afterwards, three men of the 9th Company had already been killed by a shot in the head at this harmless looking spot. That same afternoon, I was lured out of my bunker, where I was sitting comfortably reading at the coffee table. The shooting was not particularly strong at the moment. Up ahead, barrage signs rose steadily. From the returning wounded I deduced that the English had penetrated the main line of resistance in sections B and C, and the apron in A. The enemy had been in the area. Immediately thereafter came the unfortunate news that Lieutenants Vorbeck and Grieshaber had been killed defending their sections, and that Lieutenant Kastner had been seriously wounded. At 8 o'clock, Lieutenant Sprenger, who had been leading the 5th Company by proxy, also came to my dugout with a splinter in his back, regained his strength with a "look down the tube" and went to the dressing station with the quotation: "Backward, backward, Don Rodrigo." He was followed by his friend, Lieutenant Domeyer, with a bleeding hand.

The next morning we relieved the crew of Section C, which in the meantime had been cleared of the enemy. There I found Pioneers Boje and Kius with a part of the 2nd Company, Gipkens with the remains of the 9th Company. In the trench lay eight dead Germans and two Englishmen (badge on the helmets read: South-Africa, Otago-Rifles). All were badly battered by hand grenade hits. Their fear-distorted faces showed terrible injuries. Two of the men had both of their eyes shot out.

As I greeted Boje and Kius in our usual pessimistic-ironic tone, I felt the horrified eyes of one of my recruits, a seminarian, staring right through me. I could sense his train of thought and was thoroughly shocked for the first time by the deadening effect of the war. One came to regard man only as a thing.

I had the barricade occupied and the trench cleared. At 11:45 a.m., without any prior notice, our own artillery opened a furious fire on the position in front of us, but we received more hits than the English.

The disaster was not long in coming. The cry "Medic!" flew through the trench from the left. Rushing in, I found a shapeless mass of corpses in front of the barricade in the Hedge Trench, along with the remains of my best platoon leader. He had received a direct hit from one of his own grenades in the middle of his back. Scraps of uniform and underwear, torn from his body by the pressure of the explosion, hung above him in the chopped branches of a hawthorn hedge. I had a canvas thrown over him to spare the men the sight. Immediately afterwards, three more men were wounded at the same spot, one of them having both hands pierced at the joint. He staggered back with his face as pale as death, his arms resting on the shoulders of a stretcher bearer, covered in blood. Fusilier Ehlers was squirming on the ground, stunned by the air pressure.

I sent protest after protest to the command posts, urgently demanding cessation of fire or the presence of artillery officers in the trench. Instead of any response, another heavy caliber shell was launched, turning the trench into a meat bank. Blood, brains and scraps of flesh lay everywhere, with swarms of flies gathering on them.

At 7:15 a.m., I received an order stating that strong artillery fire would begin at 7:30 a.m., and that two groups of the assault company under Lieutenant Voigt were to break through the barricade of the Hedge Trench at 8 a.m., in an effort to roll up to Red Point A and to connect to the right with a parallel advancing shock troop. Two groups of my company were to follow to occupy the captured section of the trench.

While the artillery fire was already beginning, I hurriedly made the necessary arrangements and designated two groups. I spoke briefly with Lieutenant Voigt, who proceeded a few minutes later in accordance with orders. I considered the matter more of an evening stroll and walked behind my two groups, with my cap on my head and a hand grenade under my arm. At the moment of the attack, the rifles of the whole area were aimed at the Hedge Trench. We jumped, while hunched over, from parapet to parapet. We advanced forward very nicely and the English escaped to their rear line leaving one dead.

I was the last to pass the junction of a trench branching off to the left when the man in front of me, a non-commissioned officer, let out a scream of the utmost excitement and shot past my head to the left. Since I could not explain his behavior, I took a few steps back and suddenly found myself face to face with an athletically built Englishman, and at that very moment he hurled a hand grenade at the fleeing NCO. At the same time, the screams of attack from some more Englishmen rang out from all sides as they rushed over cover to cut us off. I pulled out my hand grenade, my only weapon, and hurled it at the Tommy's feet. Then, knocked down by hand grenades, I set off in the direction of our trench. Only one, little Wilzek from my company, had the prudence to run after me. An iron egg that was thrown at us tore his belt and the seat of his pants without injuring him further.

Voigt and the other men who had dodged to the front seemed surrounded and lost. Battle cries and numerous explosions announced that they were selling their lives dearly.

In order to come to their aid, I led Fahnenjunker-Unteroffizier Mohrmann's group through the Hedge Trench. In the meantime we had to stop in front of a barrage of hail-proof bottle mines. A piece of shrapnel flew against my chest and was caught by my suspenders buckle. In addition, an artillery barrage of enormous strength broke out abruptly.

Fountains of earth and colored vapors splashed all around, metallic blasts screamed through the dull drum roll of heavy blows, iron blocks roared in with uncanny brevity, clouds of shrapnel sang and whirred in between. Since an attack appeared to be imminent, I put on a random steel helmet that was lying on the ground and hurried back to the battle trench with some companions.

On the other side, figures appeared. We laid down on the parapet and fired. Next to me, a very young warrior, with feverish hands, fiddled with the loading lever of his jammed machine gun without managing to get a single shot out of the barrel. Some Englishmen folded over, the others disappeared into the trench, while the fire became more and more extreme. Our artillery seemed to be unable to differentiate between their own men and the enemy.

As I strode to my bunker, followed by a battle orderly, something slammed into the wall between us, ripping my steel helmet off my head with enormous force and hurling it far away. I thought I had received a whole load of shrapnel and laid down half-stunned in my foxhole, on the edge of which a shell struck a few seconds later, filling the small room with dense agony. A long piece of shrapnel shattered a can of cucumbers lying beside my feet. To avoid being buried, I crawled back into the trench and spurred the two battle orderlies and my lad to vigilance.

It was a really unpleasant half hour, during which the company suffered many casualties. After the wave of fire had died down, I went through the trench, surveyed the damage and determined how many men I still had at my disposal. Since the head count of fifteen men was too low for linear defense, I put Fahnenjunker Mohrmann and three men in charge of defending the barricade, pulled the debris together into a firing hedge in a giant crater behind my own line, and had all the hand grenades piled there. My plan was to let the attacking enemy come quietly into the trench, then smash them together from above at the sound of a whistle. However, combat activity was limited to a continual skirmish with light shells, rifles and hand grenades.

On July 27th, we were relieved by a company of the 164th Infantry Regiment. We were also completely exhausted. The leader of this company was severely wounded on the approach; a few days later my bunker was shelled, burying his successor. We all breathed a sigh of relief when we had Puisieux in our rear, where the storms of steel of the great final offensive were beginning its wrath.

*　　*　　*　　*　　*　　*

111th Infantry Division

Divisional Headquarters,
12/08/1918

DIVISIONAL ORDERS OF THE DAY

The 73rd Fusilier Regiment has once again brilliantly proven its high reputation as a brave, battle-tested troop in the hard battles on the 25th of July, against an enemy far superior in numbers, in defense and counterattacks. I acknowledge this all the more gladly, as I am well aware of the high demands that must be placed on the troops of the division in terms of endurance and devotion to duty for our beloved fatherland during the long deployment on the difficult front.

In particular, Lieutenant Jünger, already wounded six times and this time, as always, a shining example for officers and enlisted men, deserves renewed recognition.

VON BUSSE,
Major-General and Division Commander

XIX

My Last Storm

ON July 30, 1918, we moved into the resting quarters of Sauchy-Léstrée, a watery pearl of Artois. After a few days, we marched even further back to Escaudoeuvres, a small, sober working-class suburb of Cambrai.

I inhabited the typical state room of a northern French worker's cottage in the Rue-des-Bouchers. The usual giant bed as the ominous main piece of furniture, a fireplace with hideous red and blue glass vases on the shelf, a round table, chairs; on the walls some of the awful color prints of Familistère, Vive la classe, souvenir de première communion, postcards and other junk. All together the height of mendacious sentimentality and uncomfortableness. I felt more uncomfortable in the midst of this self-indulgent tastelessness than in the wettest of dugouts, and tried to at least motivate my presence somewhat with some playing cards stacked on the table and my riding boots slung on the family bed.

The bright full moon nights favored frequent visits by enemy planes, which gave us an idea of the overwhelming material superiority on the opposite side. Night after night several squadrons swooped in and dropped bombs of an unearthly explosive power on Cambrai and the suburbs. I was disturbed less by the fine, mosquito-like hum of the motors and the clusters of long echoing detonations than by the anxious rushing into the cellar of my landlords. One day before my arrival, however, a bomb had exploded outside the window, riddling the walls with shrapnel, and knocking my landlord, who was sleeping in my bed, into the other room, stunned. This very incident, however, reassured me that a repetition would be quite unlikely.

After a day of rest, the hated but indispensable training lecture resumed. Drill, lessons, roll calls, meetings and visits filled a large part of the day. We even spent an entire morning in an honorable court sentence. The food was once again miserable. For a while, the only evening portion was cucumbers, to which the dry humor of the people gave the apt name "gardener's sausages."

It was not easy to fuse my decimated company back into a unit. Even though the necessity was clear to me, I often found it embarrassing to have to keep on approaching the men with the trivialities of drill. Drill cannot be dispensed with as a means to an end in any army; it cannot be entirely replaced by either individual or sports education. A man whose inner worth is not beyond all doubt must learn to obey to the point of stupor, so that even in the most terrible moments his impulses can be restrained by the spiritual compulsion of the leader.

Above all, I devoted myself to the training of a shock troop, since in the course of the war it had become increasingly clear to me that all success springs from the deed of the individual, while the mass of followers represents only shock and firepower. I would rather be the leader of a determined group than of a timid company.

I spent my free time reading, bathing, shooting and riding. On the rides I found masses of leaflets thrown down to accelerate the process of moral decomposition of our army. There was even a poem by Schiller about free Britain. I thought it was quite clever of the English to bombard the German mind with poems, and also quite flattering for us. A war in which people fight each other through verse would be quite a beneficial invention. The premium award of thirty pfennigs per copy found revealed that the army command did not underestimate the dangerousness of these poisonous weapons. The expenses, however, were charged to the population of the occupied area. It seemed that we no longer had a pure understanding of poetry after all.

One afternoon, I got on my bike and rode to Cambrai. The dear old town had become desolate and barren. Stores and cafes were closed; the streets seemed dead despite the field-gray surge that flooded them. I found Mr. and Mrs. Plancot, who had given me such fine quarters the year before, cordially pleased with my visit. They told me that conditions in Cambrai had deteriorated in every respect. In particular, they complained about the frequent air raids, which forced them to run up and down the stairs several times at night, arguing over the problem of whether it was more advisable to perish in the first cellar by the bomb itself or in the second cellar by being buried alive. I felt very sorry for the old men, with their worried expressions. A few weeks later, as a result of the bombardment, they had to leave, head over heels, the house in which they had spent their lives.

On August 23rd, at about 11 o'clock, I was woken up, having just fallen into a very pleasant sleep, by a heavy pounding against my door. It was an orderly bringing me the marching orders. Since the day before the monotonous rolling and pounding of an unusually heavy artillery fire had blazed over from the front. We took this as a warning, while on duty, eating and playing cards, not to entertain any illusions as to a longer rest period. We had coined the sonorous front expression "it booms" for this bubbling of distant cannon thunder.

We quickly packed up and started on the road to Cambrai under the roar of a heavy thunderstorm. Our marching destination was Marquion, where we arrived at about 5:00 a.m. The company was assigned a large yard enclosed by a row of demolished stable buildings, in which everyone accommodated himself as best he could. I crawled with my only company officer, Lieutenant Schrader, into a small brick dungeon that had apparently functioned as a goat pen in more peaceful times, but was now only inhabited by a few large rats.

In the afternoon, there was an officers' meeting at which we learned that we were to be made ready during the night on the right of the great Cambrai-Bapaume road, not far from Beugny. We were also warned of a possible attack by the newer, faster and more maneuverable enemy tanks.

I divided my company for the battle in a small orchard. Standing under an apple tree, I spoke a few words to the men who surrounded me in a horseshoe. Their faces looked serious and manly. There was little to say. Everyone knew that we could no longer win the war. But the enemy should see that he was fighting against men of honor.

On such occasions, I avoided being carried away by bravado. It would not have been very tactful to show the men, some of whom were heading to annihilation while also fearing for their wives and children, that I was looking forward to the battle with a certain amount of pleasure. It was also my principle not to incite the mute or threaten the coward with big words. I suggested: "I know very well that no one will leave me in the lurch. We are all afraid, but we have to fight against it. It is human when someone is overcome by his weakness. He must then look to his leader and his comrades." Even while speaking, I felt that such words were understandable to men. The successes brilliantly justified this psychological preparation.

In the courtyard, at our table, which was basically a front door laid on top of a cart, Schrader and I ate dinner and shared a bottle of wine. Then we rested in our goat pen until 2 a.m., when the guard told us that the trucks were ready to be loaded at the marketplace.

Under a ghostly illumination, we rattled through the battle-scarred terrain of last year's Battle of Cambrai and wound our way through the village streets. Close to Beugny, we were unloaded and led to our assembly areas. The battalion occupied a valley on the Beugny-Vaux road. In the morning hours, an orderly brought the order for the company to advance to the Frémicourt-Vaux road. This typical advance convinced me that we were in for some bloodshed before nightfall.

I snaked my three platoons through the perilous terrain, which circling planes regularly pounded with bombs and shells. At the appointed area, we scattered into craters and holes in the ground, as isolated shells reached beyond the road.

I was in such a bad way that day that I immediately laid down in a small trench and fell asleep. After awakening, I read Laurence Sterne's "Tristram Shandy" and spent the afternoon lying in the warm sun with the indifference of a sick person. Now and then I drank a sip of vermouth.

At 6:15 in the afternoon, an orderly called the company commanders to visit with Captain von Weyhe. "I have an important notice: we are attacking. The battalion, after an artillery preparation of half an hour, will start the assault at 7 o'clock from the western edge of Favreuil. Marching point will be the church tower of Sapignies."

After a short back and forth and a strong handshake, we rushed to the companies, since the firing was to begin in ten minutes and we still had a long distance to march. I informed my platoon leaders and ordered them to line up.

"Groups line up in single file with twenty meters between each man. March left to the treetops of Favreuil!"

An excellent sign that the spirit was still in the men was that when I had to assign one man with the duty of staying behind to notify the field kitchen — no one volunteered.

I walked far ahead of the column with my company staff and Sergeant Reinecke, who knew the area well. The firing of our artillery started up behind hedges and ruins. The fire resembled more of an angry yelp than a devastating storm wave. Behind me I saw my groups proceeding in perfect order. Beside them small clouds of smoke accumulated from the shells dropped from the airplanes, bullet charges, hollow points and pieces of shrapnel were darting with infernal roars through the interstices of the narrow strips of men. On the right lay the heavily shelled Beugnâtre, from which jagged pieces of iron whirred over slowly and punched into the loamy ground with a short blow.

The advance behind the Beugnâtre-Bapaume road became even more uncomfortable. Suddenly, a series of brisance grenades exploded in front, behind and between us. We scattered apart and threw ourselves into the craters. I accidentally plunged my knee into a the corpse of a predecessor and, in a hurry, had my lad clean me up with a knife.

The clouds of numerous impacts clustered around the edge of the village of Favreuil, in between brown fountains of earth sprang up and fell in hasty alternation. To orientate myself, I went ahead alone to the first set of ruins and then gave the sign to follow with the walking stick.

The village was surrounded by bullet-riddled barracks, where parts of the 1st and 2nd Battalions were gradually gathering. On the last section of the road, a machine gun claimed several victims. Among others, Vice Sergeant Balg of my company received a shot through the leg. A figure in a brown Manchester suit strode indifferently over the shelled terrain and shook my hand. Kius and Boje, Captain Junker and Schaper, Schrader, Schläger, Heins, Findeisen, Höhlemann and Hoppenrath stood behind a hedge swept by lead and iron to prepare the attack. On many a day of wrath we had fought on one field, and this time, too, the sun, already low in the west, will illuminate the blood of almost everyone.

Parts of the 1st Battalion moved into the castle park. Of the 2nd Battalion, only my company and the 5th Company had passed through the flaming curtain in full force. We worked our way through craters and house debris to a valley on the western edge of the village. On the way, I put a steel helmet I had found on my head, an action I used to perform only at critical moments. To my amazement, Favreuil seemed to be completely deserted, the crew had apparently abandoned their defensive section.

Captain von Weyhe, who was already lying lonely and badly wounded in a crater of the village, had ordered that the 5th and 8th Companies should storm in the front line, the 6th in the second line and the 7th in the third line. Since there was still nothing to be seen of the 6th and 8th Companies, I decided to move on without worrying much about the prearranged echelons.

It was now 7 o'clock. Through the backdrop of remnants of houses and tree stumps, I saw a line of riflemen step out onto the open field under faint rifle fire. It had to be the 5th Company. I lined up my men in the valley and gave orders to move in two waves. "Distance, one hundred meters! I myself will be between the first and second wave."

We set out on our last storm. How many times in the past years we had strode into the western sun in a similar mood! Les Eparges, Guillemont, St. Pierre-Vaast, Langemarck, Paschendale, Moeuvres, Braucourt, Mory! Another bloody feast beckoned.

We left the valley somewhat according to plan, only "I myself," as the beautiful command formula reads, suddenly found myself next to Lieutenant Schrader far ahead of the first wave.

Isolated rifle shots rang out towards us. Walking stick in my right hand, pistol in my left, I trudged forward and, without really noticing

197

it, left the firing line of the 5th Company partly behind me to my right. As I proceeded, I noticed that my Iron Cross had come loose from my chest and fallen to the ground. Schrader, my lad, and I began to search diligently, even though concealed riflemen seemed to be targeting us. Finally, Schrader pulled it out of a patch of grass, and I pinned it back in place.

The terrain was downhill. Blurred figures moved against a background of brown clay. A machine gun unloaded its bullet sheaves at us. I was gripped by a fatal feeling of hopelessness. Nevertheless, we began to run. In the middle of jumping over a trench, a piercing blow to the chest tore me out of the air. With a loud scream, I was spun around and clattered to the ground, stunned.

I awoke to a sense of great misfortune, sandwiched between tight mud walls, while the call, "Medic! The company commander is wounded!" slid through a crouched line of men.

An older man from another company bent over me with a good-natured face, untied the belt and opened my coat. Two bloody circular stains shone from the center of the right breast and from the back. A feeling of paralysis bound me to the earth, and the glowing air of the narrow trench bathed me in agonizing sweat. The compassionate older man cooled me down by fanning me with my map case. While gasping for air, I hoped that it would be dark soon so that I could be dragged to the back.

Suddenly, a hurricane of fire roared in from Sapignies. It was clear that this nonstop drumming, this steady roar and pounding was intended for more than to just repel our poorly timed attack. I looked into Lieutenant Schrader's face hovering above me, petrified under his steel helmet, who fired and fired, like a machine. A conversation developed between us that was reminiscent of the tower scene in Tchaikovsky's The Maid of Orleans. I was not in a very humorous mood, however, since I had the clear realization that I was done for.

Above, cries of terror went from mouth to mouth: "They've broke through on the left! We've been bypassed!" It gave me back my old strength. I grasped a hole that a mole had bored in the trench wall and pulled myself up while blood trickled from my wounds. With my head bare, my coat open and my pistol in my fist, I stared into the fray.

Through whitish clouds of smoke, a chain of packed men plunged straight ahead. Some fell and remained on the ground, others cartwheeled like hit hares. A hundred meters ahead, the last ones were sucked in by the crater terrain.

As if pulled by a string, four tanks crawled over the top of a hill. A few minutes later they were pounded into the earth by the artillery. One of them folded in half like a tin toy. On the right, the brave Fahnenjunker Mohrmann collapsed with a death cry.

The situation did not seem lost yet. I whispered to Ensign Wilsky to crawl to the left and sweep the gap with his machine gun. He returned immediately and reported that everyone had already surrendered twenty meters ahead. Parts of 99th Regiment (Zabern) were lying there. Turning around, I witnessed a strange sight. Men were coming forward from behind with their hands up! The enemy must have already taken the village from which we had stormed.

The scene became more and more animated. A circle of Englishmen and Germans surrounded us and asked us to throw down our weapons. In a weak voice, I encouraged those closest to me to fight with the knife. They shot at friend and foe. A circle of silent and screaming figures surrounded our little group. On the left, two hulking Englishmen plunged their bayonets into a trench from which pleading hands stretched out.

Valid voices were also raised among us: "It's no use anymore! Put down your rifles! Don't shoot, comrades!"

I glanced at the two officers standing in the trench with me. They smiled back fatalistically and dropped their belts to the ground.

The choice remained between captivity and a bullet. Now the moment had come to show whether what I had told my men in many a day of rest about the battle was more than empty phrases. I crawled out of the trench and staggered toward Favreuil. Two Englishmen, leading a squad of captured 99ers toward their lines, confronted me. I held my pistol to the nearest one and pulled the trigger. He collapsed like a shooting gallery figure. The other fired his rifle at me without hitting. The hasty movements caused another leakage of blood from my lungs. I was able to breathe more freely and began to walk along the trench section. Behind a parapet, Lieutenant Schläger crouched in the midst of a firing group of men. They joined in. Some Englishmen striding across the compound stopped, put a Lewis rifle on the ground and fired at us. Everyone was hit except Schläger, two companions and myself. Schläger, who had lost his pince-nez glasses, told me later that he had seen nothing but my map case flying up and down. The constant loss of blood gave me the freedom and ease of intoxication; I was only worried by the thought of collapsing too soon.

At last, we came to a crescent-shaped mound of earth to the right of Favreuil, from which half a dozen heavy machine guns were spewing fire at friend and foe. Enemy shells splattered in the sand of the trench, officers shouted, excited men danced back and forth. A medical sergeant of the 6th Company tore off my jacket and advised me to lie down immediately, otherwise I might bleed to death in a few minutes.

I was rolled into a tent canvas and dragged along the outskirts of Favreuil. Some of my men and men of the 6th Company accompanied me. After a few hundred paces we received rifle fire from the village at close range. Bullets slammed into bodies. The medic of the 6th Company, who was carrying the rear end of my tent, was knocked to the ground by a shot to the head; I fell with him.

The small flock had thrown themselves smoothly to the ground and crawled, whipped around by impacts, towards the nearest depression in the ground. I remained lonely, tied up in my tent in the field, waiting for the final hit. But as long as one man of my company was still alive, I was not completely abandoned. Next to me the voice of Fusilier Hengstmann rang out: "I'll take the Lieutenant on my back, either we get through or we stay down."

Unfortunately, we did not get through; too many guns were aimed at us on the outskirts of the village. As I sat on his back with my arms wrapped around his neck, a fine metallic whizzing sound rang out. Hengstmann sank very gently under me. I released myself from his arms, which still held my thighs tightly. A bullet had pierced his steel helmet and temples. The brave man who sealed his loyalty to his leader with death was a teacher's son from Letter, near Hanover. I later visited his family and hold his memory sacred.

The terrible instance did not deter another helper from making a new attempt to rescue me. It was the medical sergeant Strichalsky. He took me on his shoulders and happily brought me to the blind spot of the nearest fold in the ground.

Darkness was falling. My loyal companions took a dead man's canvas and carried me across a lonely terrain where jagged stars flamed up near and far. I had to gasp for air, one of the most agonizing feelings a man can have. The scent of a cigarette smoked by a man ten steps in front of me almost suffocated me.

Finally, we reached a bandage shelter, where Doctor Key, a friend of mine, was doing his duty. He mixed me a delicious lemonade and sank me into a refreshing slumber with a morphine injection.

The next day, the usual, stage-by-stage return transport began. The desolate car ride to the war hospital brought me to the edge of my grave. Then I came into the hands of the nurses. Although I am not a misogynist, the feminine nature irritated me every time the fate of battle threw me into the bed of a hospital room. From the masculine, purposeful and purposive action of war one plunged into an atmosphere of indefinable emanations. A pleasant exception was the detached objectivity of the Catholic nuns.

After fourteen days, I laid in the springy bed of a hospital train and was lucky enough to be unloaded in Hannover. There I laid in the Clementine Convent together with a young fighter pilot of the Richthofen Squadron, who had already downed twelve opponents in an air fight. The last one had shattered his humerus bone with a bullet. On our first recovery walk we met my brother and some comrades, with whom we had dinner. Since our imminent fitness for war was being questioned, we both felt the unconditional need to exercise over a huge armchair. Nevertheless, we soon felt in shape for a new winter campaign. This was postponed for the time being. We were soon to take part in other battles that we couldn't have dreamed of.

On September 22, 1918, I received the following telegram from General von Busse:

"His Majesty the Emperor has awarded you the Order Pour le Mérite. I congratulate you on behalf of the entire division."